Praise for …

STREET PASTO.

"Les Issac's story of how he founded and developed Street Pastors is an example of faith in action and emblematic of building up the kingdom of God. *Street Pastors* works because it recognises both our common humanity and common responsibility in bringing hope to the communities we share. This story should serve as a source of inspiration for all who work to restore society, to raise the fallen and to help our young people know the warmth of God's love and welcome."

Dr. John Sentamu, Archbishop of York

"Street Pastors is a wonderful example of local people actively taking care of other local people. The commitment and energy shown by individual pastors on a regular basis is truly inspiring. As a senior police officer and as a parent, I am enormously grateful for their work in keeping vulnerable people safe and preventing potential problems from occurring later in the evening.

"I have seen firsthand the supportive relationships that exist between local police officers, special constables, police community support officers and street pastors—each recognising the value the other brings. There are so many stories of the impact street pastors have made and continue to make within our cities and towns."

Olivia Pinkney,
assistant chief constable, Sussex Police

STREET PASTORS

LES ISAAC

WITH ROSALIND DAVIES

David C Cook®

transforming lives together

STREET PASTORS
Published by David C. Cook
Kingsway Communications LTD
Lottbridge Drove, Eastbourne BN23 6NT, England

David C. Cook
4050 Lee Vance View, Colorado Springs, CO 80918 U.S.A.

David C. Cook Distribution Canada
55 Woodslee Avenue, Paris, Ontario, Canada N3L 3E5

Survivor is an imprint of David C. Cook
Kingsway Communications Ltd
info@survivor.co.uk

David C. Cook and the graphic circle C logo
are registered trademarks of Cook Communications Ministries.

Scripture quotations are taken from the *Holy Bible, New International Version*®.
NIV®. © 1973, 1978, 1984 by the International Bible Society. Used by permission
of Zondervan. All rights reserved. Scripture quotations marked ESV are taken from
The Holy Bible, English Standard Version. Copyright © 2000; 2001 by Crossway
Bibles, a division of Good News Publishers. Used by permission. All rights reserved.

ISBN 978-1-84291-419-9

The Team: Richard Herkes, Amy Kiechlin, Jaci Schneider, and Karen Athen
Cover Design: Dan Armstrong, www.wildfirestudio.co.uk

Printed in the United States of America
First Edition 2009

1 2 3 4 5 6 7 8 9 10

082609

CONTENTS

The title for each chapter is taken from a newspaper or newsletter headline or article. The title of the publication is listed under the chapter titles throughout the book.

ACKNOWLEDGEMENTS

The past eight years have been both challenging and privileged. It has been a humbling experience to see and meet the many people from all walks of life and denominations who want to become street pastors. Many have been a source of encouragement and strength, helping me stay focused and determined so that we can all make a difference to our communities.

First and foremost I want to thank my Lord Jesus, in whom I place my hope. My heartfelt thanks goes to my wife, Louise, my son, Jake, and my daughter, Lara, without whose unstinting support and encouragement I would not be able to do what I do. My thanks also go to the late Davidson Stoute, Major Jo Norton and Regina Ochei for their inspiration and unwavering commitment to me.

I would like to express my thanks to all street pastors. I am grateful for each and every one of you. Thank you, also, those of you who have contributed your stories to this book.

I would also like to acknowledge and thank my co-founders, the Reverend David Shosanya and Detective Constable Ian Crichlow for their contribution to the development of the Street Pastors concept. I am grateful to David for the many nuggets of wisdom he has allowed me to quote in this book. To the board of trustees, led by Julaine Hedman, I would also like to express my gratitude, for their support and encouragement and for their willingness to engage with all the complexities involved in this work.

Thank you to all members of my staff at Ascension Trust, capably led by Eustace Constance, for their commitment and willingness to go the extra mile. I want to acknowledge the work of all the Street Pastors management committees and coordinators around the country, for their vision for each local area and their desire to serve their community. To all those who train street pastors I would also like to express my thanks. It is vital that all trainees be properly equipped for the role of street pastors, and your work is very much appreciated. I would also like to commend the first set of street pastors to walk the streets, in particular Reverend Herma Butler and Reverend Joyce Daley.

I want to thank Oliver Nyumbu, chief executive of Caret, and his team for their generosity and support over the years, helping us to develop the training strategy and structure to enable the growth of the initiative. Also the various newspapers, the independent think-tanks, the Centre for Crime and Justice, local government publications and committee reports, *Metropolitan Police* magazine, that post their work on the Internet.

I am especially grateful to the various police press and publicity officers for approving the publication of comments from officers. For permission to quote from his PhD thesis, my thanks are due to Paul Keeble, and for their willingness to allow us to refer to their independent evaluation reports, I am grateful to Peter Cornish and G. S. Burgess and Co.

INTRODUCTION TO STREET PASTORS

by Ram Gidoomal

I first met Les Isaac in an elevator. We were both invited guests on our way to Premier Radio, and in the elevator he pitched to me, in one minute, the idea of Street Pastors. He did such a good job that when we went into the studio to do the interview, I was the one plugging the initiative!

At the time of my first meeting with Les, the government was talking a lot about crime and the causes of crime. I believe that Street Pastors is an initiative that can help reduce crime and also address the causes of crime. I have talked about Street Pastors with many groups, and when I was a candidate in the London mayoral and assembly elections in 2000 and 2004, the Street Pastors initiative was very much part of my own campaign. It wasn't just words: to the extent that I had political influence, I wanted to promote it.

Street Pastors is an amazingly practical, hands-on response to the problems our communities face, and it is one of the best ideas that I have seen emerge in recent years. It is a simple yet innovative and cost-effective idea. It is tackling the ills that face local communities, and when we talk of solving the problems of the nation, we need to realise that they distil down to local communities.

As the name implies, the Street Pastors initiative operates literally at street level, offering a local solution to problems which at national level seem insurmountable: through it policymakers can think national and act local. We are also beginning to see the international scope of this very simple and powerful initiative. It is demonstrating that it is worthy of global consideration, and as it does so, it brings reality to the slogan 'Think global and act local'.

As a businessman I know that a key measure of the success of any good idea is reproducibility across different contexts. Street Pastors delivers this. I am, of course, a fan of the initiative, its wholehearted endorser and delighted to support it as a patron.

Ram Gidoomal CBE, patron of Street Pastors
Chairman, Citylife Industrial and Provident Society Ltd
Chairman, South Asian Concern Charitable Trust

FOREWORD

by David Burrowes

I first heard of Street Pastors when I was a local councillor in Enfield. I attended the inaugural meeting in the Civic Centre with low expectations of another social action initiative. I then encountered Les Isaac! His enthusiasm and passion for Street Pastors was infectious.

Many books fill our shelves telling us why Christians should be involved in their communities, but this book provides an answer to the question of how. The Street Pastors initiative is a fine example of Christians being present at street level and drawing alongside others, helping and guiding them in their needs, rather than just talking about the issue. Throughout the country, week in and week out, Christians are being beacons for compassion and concern—whether they are pointing people in the right direction, persuading someone not to do something, or being a shoulder to cry on. Yet this book goes beyond recounting the immense contribution of Street Pastors. It challenges us all to follow its example, to build good relationships with partners outside the church while maintaining distinctive and strong Christian foundations.

The Street Pastors initiative represents many different denominations and helps churches to see their work as something that goes beyond simply having a meeting or project. Churches can be practically involved with their town or city, showing the community how much the church cares for it and bringing a relevant Christian message.

This book is a tribute to Les Isaac's leadership and the success of Street Pastors as it reaches the length and breadth of the UK. I believe that the most remarkable thing about the initiative is the way street pastors are bridging the gap between the community and people in authority, and in this sense this is a book more about partners than individuals: partnerships with the Home Office, police, churches and the community.

As a Christian MP, with an interest in the area of criminal justice and policing, and a patron of Street Pastors, it is not surprising that I support Street Pastors. However, the support from parliamentary colleagues of different political and religious affiliations highlights the growing influence of the initiative.

This book is a testament to several things: the first steps of strong leadership, the larger steps gained through good partnerships and the countless steps on the streets by dedicated volunteers. Above all it is a testament to Street Pastors' growth and development under God, because it is, as the book of Proverbs reminds us, the Lord who determines our steps (Prov. 16:9).

David Burrowes, patron of Street Pastors
MP for Enfield Southgate and Shadow Justice Minister

DIARY OF AN ANONYMOUS STREET PASTOR

I wake up early. The day will be a busy one. Rain is forecast for later, and I struggle to think where I last saw my waterproof trousers.

The day goes by and the rain starts. I wonder if it will mean the town will be quiet this evening. *God be in these streets tonight*, I pray silently. I get soaked as I walk around the shops looking for what I need to buy, but it actually gives me the chance to pray as I dodge the crowds, and I realise that even now, in the late afternoon, the pubs are already busy.

Later I begin to watch the clock, wishing the hands would move faster. The TV is on, but I have already left home mentally. I know I will feel less anxious when I have joined up with the others to pray. My nervous anticipation reminds me of my days in the navy, when we would wait in silence for an exercise to start. This waiting time is so strangely intense, as if the volume of the life going on around me has been turned down—even on a day like today, when there are things to be done and family all around me. I know I will go out in God's strength, but I still have all those human feelings about what will happen tonight. I know that as a street pastor I will be meeting both people who think we are the best thing since sliced bread and those who are only two or three pushes away from a fight.

Nine o'clock. I read the Met Office's severe weather warning on the Internet and smile. I'm starting to feel tired. It would be a good idea to have a nap, but I can't get off to sleep. I start to plan instead. It's too wet to cycle, so where will I park the car? My kit is ready. I eat a bowl of cereal and make a sandwich for later. I don't know what to pray and I still can't find my waterproof trousers. Will anyone be out in the town on a night like this? I say goodnight to my daughter. It's 9.20 p.m. Let's go! My wife waves me off.

It seems impossible to park. Eventually I find a space then make a dash to the church we are using as our base. There are loads of people on the streets, one man I particularly notice because he's wearing a rainbow-striped suit. I do a quick change into my uniform and pick up a handful of 'spikeys' and a pair of vinyl gloves. More people are arriving now, with everybody commenting on the weather and what a nightmare parking is tonight. I chat to a friend about what has been going on for him this week, watching the clock approach ten. We start to divvy up into teams and begin our prayer time. I feel so much better after the prayers and realise how good it is to be with people who are preparing to do the same thing as me. When we have sorted out who is carrying the kit bag, radio and phone, we are ready. I am in team B, heading for the centre of town for the first half of the night.

The first person we meet is a homeless guy. We have a chat about his welfare. There are not many people who stop to talk to someone like him. We give him a bottle of water. Then we speak to two lads and a girl who tell us they are trying to set up a project for homeless people. We encourage them as we talk. Then there is a chap who knows all about us already, and another whose sister died two years ago and who has recently been helped by street pastors in another town.

We move from one person to the next, and as always I am amazed at the number of people who are vulnerable or in need. You would think it would be just one or two, but it is so many. Conversation starts easily and the stories of their lives flood out. We meet two girls, both mums, one with a five-week-old baby at home, the other with two young children. We can see that they have already hooked up with a couple of men, and the guys want to move away down the street and are encouraging the girls to go with them. I stand back, praying all the time, as my teammate talks to them. We have to leave the girls or we'll be separated from the other pair in our team. We phone in to the prayer team and ask them to keep praying for them. We also tell them where we are heading next, and they cover that in prayer too.

We wander on slowly to another club and the door staff welcomes us, telling us to come in and meet the customers. We head for a table where Sonic the Hedgehog is having a birthday night out with Superman. Several people ask who we are.

It's 1 a.m. and time for a welcome break. Back at the base we have a cup of tea and I eat my sandwich. We go back out at 1.30 a.m. and find that the rain has stopped briefly. We have some in-depth discussions with people waiting by the burger van and have to answer some tough questions. Some want to know who we are and ask us about the existence of Jesus and God. I speak to a soldier who has recently returned from overseas. He says he is an agnostic and we get into a lengthy discussion. I encourage him to keep his mind open and he agrees to do this. We are called to various incidents by door staff. It is busy and noisy and people are everywhere. I am amazed that God directs me so clearly, almost as if He picks me up and puts me down in the places he wants me to be. As the night wears on I begin to see that He has been saying to me, 'Over there,' and, 'Over here now.'

I pray with a student from France who is studying in this country, and again with another guy, a father of two who tells me that there is no way to God for him as he has been so bad. I tell him gently that he has got God all wrong! After we have talked for a while he almost accepts Jesus right there and then, but someone else will bring him to the Lord, another time.

The clubs begin to empty. It is quite a sight. I hear some heart-rending stories. One girl tells us that she had her drink spiked while on holiday the previous year and was raped. Returning to the UK she found she was pregnant. She tells us about the abortion she has had and how she feels she is just getting herself back together. All this between two strangers on the High Street. God puts us where He wants us, sometimes just to listen.

We have picked up quite a few cans and bottles, often just following the sound of breaking glass until we find the debris. At 4 a.m. we head back to base for the debrief and prayer. My mind is absolutely buzzing and I know it will be a while before I can sleep.

After a night of rain I am able to see the sun rising as I head upstairs to bed.

CHAPTER ONE

BACK TO GRASSROOTS
The Voice, 9 August 2004

Be confident

For years Christians and non-Christians alike have thought about the streets as a realm of uncertainty, a place that represents all that is outside the peaceful and private spaces that many of us strive to create in our lives—our homes, our marriages, our families, our sanity. *Street* has become a prefix that conveys the absence of structure, a euphemism for an alternative place of belonging and identity. Our streets have swallowed up a 'generation', they are linked to loss, death and fear.[1] They need to be 'reclaimed'.[2] We are told they have become the locale for those suffering family breakdown and educational failure, those at risk of addiction and criminal behaviour.

---

1 'Losing a generation to the streets' is a feature written by Rt Hon Iain Duncan Smith MP, posted on the website of the Centre for Social Justice, an independent think-tank set up by the MP in 2004: http://centreforsocialjustice.org.uk/default.asp?pageRef=329.

2 The words of Ray Mallon, elected mayor and former senior policeman, who chaired a working group for the Centre for Social Justice which produced a report on the police, *A Force to be Reckoned With* (2009).

The streets are public places, with the potential to publicly humiliate or expose us. They can be a playground for young people, who declare in their urban 'slanguage' that they belong to this group, this scene, and the rest of us don't. In breaking out of the dance studio, 'street dance' makes use of everyday social spaces. It is not tidy and contained; it is improvisational and interactive. Our streets are also home to many rough sleepers, people for whom the sense of belonging to a place once called home has collapsed or been rejected.

In other contexts the word *street* has been adopted for its currency, for its rawness, edginess and ability to update or remarket. A quick search on the Internet shows that it is a word used by social enterprises—'StreetShine' and 'Furniture on the Street' to name but two—presumably to make such schemes appeal more to the young, disaffected people they hope to benefit. It is not surprising that the conclusion, for many, has been that the streets are no-go areas, best left to the experts.

I am profoundly grateful that Street Pastors has shown me the very opposite view.

A street pastor's response to the streets of his or her locality is very simple. A street pastor believes that the streets of our towns and cities are places of opportunity to help and care for people. This book contains many examples of how street pastors from all walks of life have greeted people nonjudgmentally and respectfully; how they have listened to them and shown them love in small acts of practical care; how they have attempted to understand rather than condemn. Street Pastors volunteers, I believe, have the potential to soften and absorb the aggression that dominates many communities and lives.

I have come to realise that many Christians have, for a long time, been living with the belief that they must be able to do something about the problems they see in their communities, but many have also lived with inaction. The Street Pastors initiative provides a structure for and the training to do what many Christians have had in their hearts and minds for years. I have heard women, in particular, say that engaging with people on the street was just something that they could not safely do alone before they became a street pastor. We have all seen drunk people, hysterical people, sad people, lonely people, and recognised in them the parallels to our own children, parents or friends. Often grandparents, of whom there are many in the Street Pastors family, say that they know their grandchildren are out and about on the streets at night; and understanding the risks they face, they want to help other young people.

And it's not just the street pastors who are ready and willing to relate to others. When I go out on the streets I always find people willing to talk to me, to have a laugh with me. Young and old who are desperate for the respectful warmth that I can convey in my handshake.

The Street Pastors scheme has helped many Christians of all ages by showing them a way in which they can earth their faith in a practical and tangible way. They can root it in the ground and see something grow from it, rather than seeing their faith float around on a theological breeze.

The church on the streets

As you read this book you will hear the sound of many authentic voices, those of street pastors from diverse communities all over Britain, police officers, politicians and church leaders. These voices are a powerful witness to the partnership of the key players in our cities—local government, the police and the church—and to the release of time, love and kingdom principles on the part of ordinary Christians. It is my hope that when Christians are active in these partnerships, confidence in the church and in our identity as Christians will grow.

As the apostle Paul says, 'I am not ashamed of the gospel, because it is the power of God for the salvation of everyone who believes' (Rom. 1:16). The gospel of our Lord Jesus Christ has brought me hope and freedom. The most exciting thing that has ever happened to me is my relationship with the Lord Jesus Christ: I am confident about my Saviour and the person He has made me.

I want to be like those first-century Christians who had a zeal and passion for Jesus. The members of the church that we read about in the book of Acts had boldness to speak about what Jesus had done for them. In them we see a strong conviction about the poor and the marginalised and how they should be loved and cared for. They had confidence that no matter how bad things were in society, something greater and better was on the horizon. When Jesus' kingdom comes, the lame will walk, the blind will see, our prisoners will be loosed and will not offend anymore. The prophecy from Isaiah that Jesus reads in Luke's gospel—'The Spirit of the Lord is on me, because he has anointed me to preach good news to the poor ...'—tells us that those in captivity, or bound by addictions, will be free (Isa. 61:1; Luke 4:18). We have got to be excited about this! We have to rekindle this degree of confidence and faith in our lives as Christians and as the church.

One night I was in Lincoln, and I watched as street pastors spoke to a nightclub owner. The man shared with them his challenges and difficulties. That man, they told me later, had declared that he hadn't darkened the door of a church for many years. Yet that night he was pouring out his heart to a street pastor. I have walked into nightclubs to find that amidst the fifteen hundred clubbers, nice refreshments are laid out for street pastors. What does this tell me? It tells me that people are saying, 'We want the church to come to us.'

Street pastors in Birmingham tell the story of a man they met in a pub who, as they chatted, told them that he used to go to church, but he had been made to choose between joining his mates in the pub and worshipping on a Sunday. From what they could gather, the man had been told by the leader of his church that he could not be a Christian if he drank alcohol. He had struggled to grasp the issues for himself, but as the street pastors spoke to him they were able to explain that although some Christians don't drink alcohol, many others do, but that they choose not to get drunk, and they could still be Christians. When the street pastors explained to this man that his friendship with God depended only on Jesus and not where he went with his mates, 'a huge grin spread across his face. It was almost as if we could see the weight being lifted off him.' This man was able to think about how to develop his relationship with Jesus, and for him, going into a church to do this would have been difficult.

We can see from this that the Street Pastors initiative provides a structure for Christians to safely engage with people on the streets, to demonstrate the love of God in a practical and tangible way. John's gospel tells us how, despite all the religious activity that was going on, the disabled man lying by the side of the pool at Bethesda couldn't get near the healing waters for thirty-eight years, until Jesus

met him and told him to pick up his bed (John 5:1–15). When we
go to people *where they are*, things happen.

God is on the move

Over the decades the church in Britain has increasingly lost contact
with organic, working-class communities. As David Shosanya, co-
founder of Street Pastors, puts it, 'Street Pastors volunteers have the
opportunity to say, "I'm going back to where I came from."' We were
not shiny and clean when we came into the church. We are who
we are today because God has done a good work in us. Therefore,
David says, 'We owe something to our communities, so that we are
not guilty of climbing the ladder and then kicking it away. We must
regain the capacity to be our brother's keeper.'

In the few years that Street Pastors has been operating, I have
discovered that it is a concept already rooted in the thinking of many
Christians. It has expressed what many have wanted to express and
given them the structure to get out and do it. So first and foremost
Street Pastors is an attitude, not a set of policies and procedures. It
has tapped into God-given certainty about the need for Christians to
look beyond themselves to others. Many new street pastors mention
a nagging sense of fear and trepidation, if not on their own part,
then from family members who are afraid they will be put in danger.
However, these same people give powerful testimonies about their
conviction to become a street pastor. They are often the ones who, on
the first night they go out, say, 'Hallelujah, I was right!'

Dressed in my Street Pastors jacket and cap, I was in a club one
night when a fight started. The bouncers started throwing people out
and the police turned up with dogs. I watched one very aggressive

man go right up to police officers, thrust his face into theirs and shout all kinds of obscenities at them. I tapped him on the shoulder. He spun round and practically spat out the words, 'Who are you?' I said, 'I'm Pastor Les.' Immediately he softened, replying, 'I'm really, really sorry.' A moment later, he turned to me again and said, 'I think you know my mum.'

There are two things we can learn from this that tell us about the essence of being a street pastor. When street pastors go out they soak up aggression. We know that when Jesus healed the man possessed by a legion of demons—a man who had become an outcast, with no control over himself and unable to be subdued by anyone else—He restored him to his community, saying 'Go home' (Mark 5:19). Street pastors can be bridge-builders between isolated or vulnerable individuals and the rest of the community. Second, street pastors find that there is a level of respect for who they are. The word *pastor* is significant. Some people, like the man I met outside the club, recognise that word. Others don't, but they will ask what it means. When they hear our answer, there is a high level of understanding of our role and the fact that a 'pastor' is there to help an individual at a time of need.

The journey so far

The story of Street Pastors as I tell it here falls into two parts: an up-to-date picture of the initiative, and its history. In presenting the current scene, the book begins by describing the kinds of people who are street pastors and explores the role and responsibilities that they take. This is more than a simple person specification, because street pastors are people who seek to understand their community at the same time as they serve it, and so a street pastor needs to grasp the bigger picture of the systemic issues that affect individuals and localities. Chapter 2 tells how our love for our communities is best articulated when we *know* our communities and, importantly, when we have learned how to be credible in our interactions with political structures and dynamics in our towns and cities.

One of the main things I hope will be of interest to many who read this book, whether they are street pastors or not, is the tremendous take-up of the initiative all over the country. The book charts how Street Pastors has progressed from its inner-city origins to the diverse contexts in which you will find it now: in regional cities, small towns, rural areas and coastal resorts. Chapter 3 paints this colourful picture and takes a look at some of the independent evaluations that we have benefited from.

The historical account begins on a personal level with my deepening awareness of God's call to engage with my community in a relevant way, and with the layers of conversation, reflection, prayer, experience, hope and fear that built a foundation for action. In order to keep working out God's plan for me I have habitually asked God what it is that He wants me to do, and I have asked myself what tools He has given me to do it.

Like a lot of things God gives us to do, this calling is always evolving. When I know what it is God wants me to do, I ask Him to provide the means for me to do it. God has provided everything I have needed.

For example, in the early days and months of the initiative, the Lord enabled me to be released from the leadership of Ichthus Christian Fellowship, and I was blessed by the support I received from that church as Street Pastors began to take shape. God also prepared someone else to take over the individual congregation in Crystal Palace, South London, for which I had responsibility and, indeed, He has brought many other people into my life at the right time.

I am grateful to God for the insights He has given me into troubled communities, and for all that I learnt when I visited Jamaica. I am amazed at the times I have seen churches working together and strangers responding to Street Pastors as God has touched their hearts. I give thanks for the moment that the trustees at Ascension Trust, the charitable organisation that operates Street Pastors, said, 'Let's go for it!' We had no money but we knew God was affirming Street Pastors as the task of this organisation.

The rest of this story, the founding of Ascension Trust, and the birth of the initiative is told in chapters 4 and 5. Although the history of Street Pastors begins here, in the guns and violence of the inner-city context, my hopes and plans for a Christian presence in our communities has taken the Street Pastors initiative from Jamaica to Jersey, from London to Lancaster. I am often asked how the original focus on gun and knife crime and serious urban issues can be relevant to other towns and cities where those things are not a feature. I have always sought to understand gun crime and gang violence not in terms of politics or criminal psychology, but in a social, economic and relational sense. I have tried to understand the broader issues, the competition, bullying, peer pressure, role modelling and the desire for belonging that vulnerable young people have to negotiate. These conditions, and the search for identity and security, are everywhere in our society.

Whatever God has called us to do, when we go beyond the realm of 'this is a good idea' and get into the realm of 'this is God's idea', He will always provide the things we need to accomplish it. In the late 1980s I began to realise that I wanted to be part of a church that spent a greater proportion of its time engaging with its locality. My congregation at Ichthus Christian Fellowship in Crystal Palace will remember the summer fêtes, making tea for people out on the street at night time, the Christmas lorry and the community barn dances! But God said to me, 'Hold on! It could be more than this. I want you to be visible; I want you to help people into jobs, to get them into rehab, to help them be reconciled with their parents.' This was how my calling began to evolve and how I realised I could listen to God and respond to Him as part of a process, not as an instant solution.

In my younger days, I preached the way to heaven. I would say, 'Come to Jesus and be saved,' and I failed to take account of the earthly condition which people might be in. I learnt that this is not actually right or biblical. The Bible says come to Jesus and He will give you life in abundance, and I believe that 'abundant life' has practical as well as spiritual implications.

A street pastor's main job is to care. Caring means being present in a physical capacity in someone else's context, in their circumstances. Street pastors listen to a person, not so that they can reply, but so that they can hear an individual's story in the knowledge that each of us is on a journey in life. Whether that person is a drug dealer, a prostitute or a child roaming the streets, a bereaved husband or an intoxicated fifteen-year-old, we are saying we want to understand how they have reached this point. Out of good listening skills comes the opportunity to help. I am very conscious that often when we see someone in need we will say, I will pray for you. I would question this, as genuine and appropriate as it may seem. Is it not shifting the responsibility for helping that person away from ourselves and onto God?

As we read the parable of the good Samaritan, we can see that helping means binding up the wound, putting someone in our own transport, seeking out the care and attention that they need and, if need be, paying the bill (Luke 10:25–37). The Samaritan knew exactly where to take the injured man so that he could be cared for. This leads me to believe that he must have had a relationship with the innkeeper, because he told the innkeeper that if there were any further costs, he should add them to his account. The Samaritan didn't (initially, at least) pay for the whole bill, so there was a level of partnership and cooperation there. 'When I return,' he said, 'I will reimburse you for any extra expense you may have' (Luke 10:35). The innkeeper cared for the man too. My feeling is that he was deeply moved by the Samaritan's generosity, and this inspired him to play his part.

Knowing how to direct a person to the appropriate care and attention is why Street Pastors is so strongly rooted in partnership. Chapters 6, 7 and 8 focus on these foundations and how I established relationships with local authorities, churches and the police in the formative years of the initiative. The challenge of helping churches to partner with each other to achieve an interdenominational response to the problems of our communities is an important part of the story of the Street Pastors initiative. I believe that Street Pastors has helped the church in Britain to rediscover its relevance in society and communities. Christian outreach and mission have often required that people publicly teach and interpret the Bible or share their faith in ways that make them feel uncomfortable. I have described how, for myself, ministry is something that evolves, and this is something that church leaders need to teach as they lead people to discover their areas of ministry.

Chapter 9 contains accounts of our 'first night' out as a team of street pastors in Brixton, South London, and conveys some of the range of emotions, experiences and encounters reported by street pastors from all over the country as they took their first steps in a Street Pastors uniform. The final chapter explores some of the challenges of expansion and some of the mechanisms we have put in place to facilitate growth.

CHAPTER TWO

FLIP-FLOP ANGELS
Church Times, 30 January 2009

Know your community

Street pastors provide practical help and advice to those at risk of involvement in antisocial behaviour or crime. Their presence and relationships with people on the street expresses the closeness of street pastors to their community, as well as their early awareness of local issues; both qualities that statutory agencies find difficult to replicate.

In a report on the overrepresentation of young black people in the criminal justice system, the Home Affairs Committee noted the valuable role of faith-based groups in reducing this imbalance. Throughout the committee's inquiry into a variety of voluntary initiatives, it found that proximity to the local community was a huge strength. In the case of Street Pastors in particular, the committee noted that its nationwide growth was compatible with the preservation of local knowledge and understanding.[1]

> The majority of people seem to have understood that we are there in a nonjudgmental, voluntary capacity to bring worth to people. When they see us in action with drunk, frightened, beaten-up people, they quickly cotton on to what we are about. We have people of all ages thanking us for being here.
>
> *Street pastor, Plymouth*

Street Pastors teams record information about the type and extent of their activities, and when that is collated over a period of several months it gives us a snapshot of their community and Street Pastors' presence in it. For example, we know that in over fifty nights of patrol, Plymouth Street Pastors teams met 4,388 individuals, provided reassurance to 121 people who needed protection, dealt with 3 racist incidents, 25 nonracial assaults, and called the ambulance 8 times. They helped 451 homeless people and talked with 1,049 door staff.[2] Street pastors in Kingston, Surrey, analysed data collected over a sixteen-week period in 2007, which tell us that during this time they attended 41 conflict situations and met 1,260 people, mostly aged between 18 and 25.[3] In Torbay, over eight nights out on the streets in February 2009, street pastors made 530 contacts with people and attended 24 incidents.[4]

---

1   House of Commons Home Affairs Committee, Second Report of Session 2006–7, 'Young Black People and the Criminal Justice System', vol. 1, p. 67.
2   In Plymouth there are a total of 89 street pastors, and a further 150 'prayer pastors' in the prayer team.
3   Figures published in *Reform*, the magazine of the United Reformed Church, April 2007.
4   Torbay Street Pastors' Spring Newsletter 2009.

Over sixteen weeks, we removed 1,366 bottles/glasses
(1,366 fewer weapons available for use in fights).

Street Pastors, Kingston

Over fifty nights of patrols:

Flip-flops given away, 276

Emergency blankets given out, 46

Bottles collected, 4,868

Distance covered by street pastors each night on average,
7 miles

Street Pastors, Plymouth

From October 2008 to February 2009:

Nights out on the streets, 67

Bottles/glass removed, 1,232

Umbrellas collected, 90

Emergency blankets given out, 61

Bandages applied, 16

Water bottles handed out, 115

Flip-flops distributed, 258

Street Pastors, Torbay

After each evening I always feel that the team (and
usually I, personally) have not wasted our time, that we
were useful—even if the effects cannot be scientifically
measured and some we will probably never know. We

are simply there to care and listen, bringing and keeping
peace.

Street pastor, Kingston

This conjunction of faith and action is powerful for so many: for
Christians, who know that faith without works is dead (James 2:17);
for onlookers, watching and waiting to see what we are all about;
and for those in our communities who need to know that someone
cares for them.

Even doing something as simple as picking up a broken
bottle helps someone—because it's one less potential
weapon on the street. I get an immensely good feeling
from helping people in this way: it's a wonderful and positive expression of my faith.

Street pastor, Westcotes

A breakdown of the service provided by one Street Pastors team
in Taunton indicates the range of things street pastors get involved
in, from requests for help from door supervisors to hosting local
MPs; from fishing a drunk person out of the river to praying for
relationship issues.

In the month of August 2008:
Free flip-flops given to barefooted people, 19
Significant conversations with individuals, 17
Significant conversations with two people or more, 9
Drunk individuals given support, 9

Prayers requested on the spot, 7

Enthusiastic responses received from clubbers, 5

Questions answered about Street Pastors, 5

Conversations with police officers, 5

Prayers for peace at tense moments, 5

Prayers for healing with individuals, 4

Foil blankets for cold people, 4

Glass and bottles removed, 4

Food obtained for hungry people, 3

Police called to situations, 3

Enjoyed company of hen/stag parties (with photos taken), 3

Conversations with staff of pubs and clubs, 2

Conversations with bus drivers, 2

Hugs and/or kisses received, 2

Street Pastors, Taunton

What kind of person is a street pastor?

Potential street pastors need to be people who know their community from the pavement up and from the council offices down. During the training course that every volunteer completes we encourage individuals to gain a knowledge of their community as a systemic whole. For street pastors there must always be a tension between the ground level expression of love—broken bottle by broken bottle— and an understanding of the political and social dynamics at work in their town or city.

Although we as Christians may have been to church in a particular neighbourhood for many years, we may not understand the various dynamics at work in that area. It can be as though we exist in another paradigm that never crosses over with any other world. David Shosanya, who wrote the session in the Street Pastors training course titled 'Knowing Your Community', says that its contents have been developed out of his personal experience and key principles and lessons he has identified.[5] 'Christians,' he says, 'often try to act in absence of knowledge or information, whereas what is needed is a sense of political literacy.'

David continues:

> In Ephesians chapter 2 Paul tells us that through Jesus Christ barriers are broken down, 'the dividing wall of hostility' is abolished (see verses 11–22, especially 14 ESV). Jesus brings the possibility of inclusion and citizenship. In Jesus we have a paradigm not just for our own access to God, but for the relationship of the 'whole building'— all parts of society—with God, and for the interpretation of spiritual truth in such a way that it is accessible for political use. I warn street pastors not to 'download' Scripture, but to find the paradigms and articulate them.

He goes on:

> I stress to Street Pastors trainees that Christians need to be more sophisticated than we often are in the way we use Scripture. For example, Christians know that there

5   I am grateful to the Revd David Shosanya for his help and inspiration in the development of the 'Knowing Your Community' section of the training, and for his contribution to the presentation of the principles of that session in this chapter.

are principalities and powers at work in communities—forces that exercise power over an area. But it would be hard for a local authority, with its humanist and secular viewpoint, to understand this. So what do we do? I argue that we need to talk about communities having different 'atmospheres' that reflect the consciousness of the people living in that area.

A mindset can be perpetuated between individuals, families and across the whole community. For example, a family in which there is long-term unemployment, where there is little expectation or motivation for change, no relationship with the children's school or other local services, will hold a mindset which will be perpetuated not just within that family but across the community. Certain beliefs build up over time and shape the default position of an area.

Another more simplistic example would be the 'broken window' scenario, where, left unrepaired, one broken window can give rise to the sense that the community is in decline. Or, more bluntly still, if you are eating a packet of crisps in an area where there are lots of empty packets discarded on the ground, what are you likely to do with *your* packet when it is finished? However, if you eat your crisps in an area which is clean and tidy, with plenty of rubbish bins around, you are more likely to deposit your empty packet in a bin.

When we acknowledge this collective consciousness
(see 2 Corinthians 10 and Ephesians 2), we can also
acknowledge that Jesus Christ intervened as a dynamic
individual to change the 'atmosphere'.

David Shosanya

'We as Christians,' David challenges, 'can do the same thing
when we engage in a relevant and appropriate way with political
and civic organisations, articulating Scripture in a politically credible
way. We can interface with communities and change them!'

What do you need to know?

The 'Knowing Your Community' training session probes the political and social literacy of trainees. You may have passion and drive,
it says, but *what do you need to know?* You plan a new initiative, but
what do you need to know? Do you know what the major trends in
community engagement have been in your area? Have you built up a
picture of how the government is addressing the problems arising in
your locality? How would you define social exclusion in your town?
During the first session of training, trainees are asked to identify the
key problems for their community. Responses indicate many common themes in diverse communities around the country. A small
sample of these would include the following:

drunk and disorderly behaviour (binge drinking culture)
twenty-four-hour licencing
youngsters with little aspiration or expectation of moving
    beyond the area

middle-aged and older people in bedsits or flats with little
   hope of improving their lives
vandalism
lack of youth facilities
lack of education
poor role models
drug misuse
aggression
homelessness
pleasure as a goal
family and relationship breakdown
fear
youth crime
loneliness
boredom
availability of weapons
gangs
racism
poor parenting
poverty
lazy churches
teenage pregnancy
truancy
domestic violence

With this basic information in place we can begin to understand the big picture and the systemic factors that influence an
individual. We are able to move from the one-dimensional label, 'a

young person who uses a knife', to the three-dimensional inquiry, 'What are the systemic issues that give rise to the person who uses a knife?' If you can start to understand these you can apply Scripture to them.

> In the early days of Street Pastors training, I used to give trainees a list of thirty questions to test their local knowledge. For example, do they know the name of the local headteacher? Where is their community library? What is the name of the leader of the council? The name of the chief superintendent of police? Who is the most senior church leader in their area? Most had no clue. So I would say to them, looking at this systemically, you are unable to engage with the most significant structures in your community. We all need to be able to back up God's discernments with information, and tangible information helps us to interpret political language and the political landscape.

> This part of the training encourages street pastors to realise that they have to be able to make connections to power brokers, even though that might be an unfamiliar world. Street pastoring is all about connecting to these power brokers. Street pastors become conduits between the structures of authority in their community and the people they meet.

> *David Shosanya*

As the training programme has developed and the initiative has grown, we are delighted to find that local police forces are very often involved in the training of new street pastors. This means that from the word *go*, street pastors are able to build an up-to-date picture of the problems facing their locality and have access to the police perspective on the dynamics of a neighbourhood.

> The training is fantastic because it puts the theoretical and the practical together. Manchester City Council Crime and Disorder Department, who are looking at long-term funding for us, have recently evaluated our Street Pastors teams, and pointed out the very high standard of our training.
>
> *Street pastor, Inner South Manchester*

A street pastor needs to be able to hold three things in tension: biblical revelation, what the Spirit is saying, and tangible information that has come from local government or the Home Office. Holding these in tension helps us to think radically about the way we use Scripture. As an introduction to the idea of a social and political re-reading of events, environments or life circumstances that we may come across as street pastors, David Shosanya directs us to the story of the good Samaritan in Luke chapter 10. Approaching the Bible with a readiness to read beneath the surface is one way we can add social and political insights to our familiar responses, in this case, our responses to the good guys and the bad guys in this story.

> In the story of the good Samaritan, it is easier to blame the robbers than interrogate the civic failings. There are,

in fact, two victims: the man who was attacked is the explicit victim, but the implicit victims are those in the gang who attacked him. We focus on the Good Samaritan as the hero, and the man who was attacked as victim, but do we ever ask whether the man travelling to Jericho was a gang member himself or whether he was attacked in revenge for something? We just assume that the man was good and the passersby and the robbers were bad.

We might ask ourselves, if the road from Jericho to Jerusalem was so bad, why was there no policing policy to minimise the risk of attack on this road? It was, in effect, a public space that had been colonised as private space by gangs. Was the road suffering from poor upkeep? Was the man attacked because the lighting along that route was insufficient? The Good Samaritan looked after the individual but did not address systemic issues, such as policing or the maintenance of local amenities.

This approach helps us to see how we can ask critical questions of an event, an environment, or an attitude. David is passionate about the need for Christians to read familiar situations from a radical perspective and go beneath the surface issues that we commonly find.

Once we begin to focus on the surface information—and don't ask deeper questions—we are romanticising the story. Jesus was answering a politically-motivated question, 'Who is my neighbour?' His answer, that the Samaritan was his neighbour, and in fact that the Samaritan could show more love than the Jew, was a fundamentally politicised answer. I believe that it is naive and disingenuous not to look at the issues that inform the answer that Jesus gave and ask the questions that are behind the question He was asked. If you are a street pastor you need to do more than just accept what appears on the surface.

When a street pastor is out on the streets he or she must think about the influences behind the choices that people make. In the case of the drug dealer, has his choice of livelihood been influenced by poor housing or a lack of education? When we meet a teenage mother, we could ask, what family circumstances has she come from that have made her want to create her own family at such an early age? What life experiences or opportunities have (or have not) been set out for her?

We can't be street pastors in a classroom, so when we are out on the streets doing the practical business of street pastoring we need to be analytical in our observations. The 'Knowing Your Community' session always includes a practical assignment of walking around the local area, so that the analytical process can be started. We could ask ourselves, what are the general trends in this community? What is the geographical layout of this area? If we see streets full of rubbish and litter, what does that tell us about the council and the community?

In some ways, this part of the Street Pastors training is designed to make us feel uncomfortable, because it makes us ask ourselves, 'This thing that I have always thought to be true, is it actually true?' It is also designed to free us from our 'spiritual' interpretations and allow us to ask questions of Scripture which we might not otherwise ask. It points out that even our spiritual experiences are limited or shaped by our personal experiences. When we read Scripture in a radically different way to the way we normally read it, it frees us up to expand our own sense of self, but also frees us to allow Scripture to speak to us in a way we have not been conditioned for it to speak to us. It is quite possible for Scripture to speak to us in this way; it is authentic. This freedom means that street pastors don't go out onto the streets and project their experience of Scripture onto someone else.

David Shosanya

Resisting stereotypes

The idea that as Christians we may be subject to 'conditioned' responses when we read the Bible or interact with people often exposes the stereotypes that we all hold. David Shosanya recalls the following examples that he has come across during training. One gentleman street pastor told us how he met a punk rocker on the street. He was a black man and had never had anything to do with punks, and when he saw that anti-establishment figure it fed into his stereotypes about punk rockers and white people. Though the punk was just a person with a different dress code, the street pastor began to pray in tongues!

In another example, a woman street pastor had been praying and believed that God had asked her to hug a young man while she was out on the streets one night. I asked her whether she was married. No, she wasn't. Had she got a boyfriend? She replied that it had been a long time since she had had a boyfriend. I challenged her by suggesting that it might be loneliness that made her hear that message from God. We carry our own baggage onto the streets, and we need to be aware of that.

White street pastors may find that they prejudge young black men who wear their trousers hanging down their backsides. The reaction might be to assume that those young men are gang members. Yet there are many black men who are in college, are committed to excellence and have clear plans for their lives. They know they need education in order to progress, but the 'resistance culture' in them says that dressing in this particular way indicates that they are different.

The Street Pastors training programme encourages people to recognise their own personal conditioning and become more self-aware. The training also draws on the basics of sociology in order to build a picture of the connectedness of social problems and antisocial behaviour. For instance, we look at issues surrounding marriage, the home and the family environment, and investigate how turmoil and conflict at home will be played out in a child's school experience. Sociology helps us to see the umbilical cord that links these things. The course is very practical; street pastors are given the knowledge to build up a picture of the underlying factors that create problems in our communities. The course gives people the tools to interpret situations and be a part of the solution.

It made me realise how judgmental we can be as people. It also made me realise what a fine line we tread with alcohol in particular. It was useful to see what we might encounter and understand some of the background problems that might exacerbate it.

Training evaluation, 'Drug and Alcohol Awareness'

Bridge-builders not preachers

The clearest message we have found we need to communicate to street pastors is that our approach is a holistic one. I know that when Christians are encouraged to go out on the streets, they will think that their task is to preach, cast out demons or pray for healing. Many Christians see that as their role outside the church. However, it is important that street pastors do not preach at people, but simply say that we care about the whole person. We must ask, 'How can we help you?' We are not there to talk about ourselves, but to listen to other people.

The first session in the training programme, 'Roles and Responsibilities', is basically a person specification. We are looking for people with a strong concern for others, those who can be bridge-builders in today's society. A bridge-builder is someone who can build a path of opportunity for another person. For example, if a person is sleeping rough, it would mean getting them into shelter; if someone is dealing drugs, helping them to walk away from that lifestyle; if some-one wants to go to church, drawing alongside to help them find their way back to church. We emphasise that we are looking for listeners, because Street Pastors is about other people, not ourselves.

Another memorable encounter was with a young man of seventeen. We had initially struck up a conversation with his friend, and while the friend was talking to another member of our team, the seventeen-year-old drew me aside and began to talk to me. He ended up telling me that his mum had been raped by her father when she was very small and it had left her with mental health issues and she was in quite a state at the moment and not coping well. His parents' marriage had broken up when he and his brother were younger. His brother, who was fifteen, was kicking over the traces and giving cause for concern, and this youngster was trying to hold it all together. He obviously felt that he had the weight of the world on his shoulders. I just said to him, 'You are doing a fantastic job,' and gave him other words of encouragement for what I saw to be a very difficult situation. He broke down and cried on my shoulder. I just held him and reassured him. What a privilege to be so trusted and accepted by these struggling youngsters.

Street pastor, Bridgend

If a young man is involved in dealing drugs, he needs to know that there is a more constructive way of earning money. So I ask the question, what has caused him to sell drugs? Is it lack of education, lack of employment opportunities, poverty or something else? In terms of carrying a gun, I need to understand why someone has decided that carrying a gun is better than not carrying a gun. Is it because that person feels threatened? Does he feel empowered when

he has a gun—becoming a 'somebody' rather than a 'nobody'? If he
is in a gang, I think: where is his family? Why is he not secure in his
family? Then I might ask myself, how do I get him out of the gang?
What do I need to do to find an exit strategy for him? For how long
do I need to support him?

> I joined Street Pastors at the end of last year and have
> had some amazing encounters with people, but there is
> one that will always remain with me. After talking to a
> young lady outside one of the pubs on a busy Saturday
> night, she said, 'You really listened, I can't believe there
> are people out there who listen. Nobody ever does
> that to me.' I didn't offer advice or have a solution but
> the gratitude was overwhelming. I thank God for those
> opportunities and pray for others like them.
>
> *Street pastor, Inverness*

The second characteristic that is important is that as street pastors we are people who can earn the right to share the gospel. When
people see that we are doing something good and credible, they will
ask us why we are doing it. Then we can explain that it is because
Christ lives in us, 'the hope of glory' (Col. 1:27). I am always looking for people whose attitude is right. People with the right attitude
will be able to engage with others, whoever and wherever they are;
whether they have faith or no faith; whatever their ethnic group;
whatever their lifestyle. There is no place for judgment or condescen-
sion, but the ability to understand another person's circumstances
is critical. Every one of us is on a journey, and we don't know how

another person has arrived at the place they are at, or why they say the things they say, or why they do what they do, or why they believe what they believe. Yet we are all human and have our own inbuilt prejudices which we have to identify and overcome. One way to do that is by making it our goal to understand where a person is coming from. The right attitude gives us the ability to 'tone down', so that we can enter into the place where people are at—whether that is a social, spiritual or cultural place. Often I see Christians with a natural inclination to be lively, bursting with a spiritual vocabulary, but to 'tone down' means that we do not focus on ourselves, but on the other person, seeking to understand them and entering into their situation.

One evening I was on the streets with some friends who were observing Street Pastors. I was verbally abused by one man for half an hour, and he was totally running down the Christian faith. I soaked up his aggression for all that time. I tried to understand where he was coming from. When I was able to get a word in, I agreed with him that we did have some things to answer for as Christians. A while later he said, 'I don't like your religion, but I do like what you're doing.' He turned and offered me and my friends hospitality, saying, 'It's cold out here. Would you like to come back to my flat? I'll give you a cup of tea and a spliff.' I jokingly replied, 'I'll have the tea, but I'll take the spliff home to my wife.' The ability to enter in is critical.

How safe are street pastors?

The idea that we might need to 'tone down' our approach also has a bearing on our safety when we are out on the streets as street pastors. Having the restraint to hold back, observe a situation, or at times, withdraw from a situation, is also a quality that volunteers need. At other times, street pastors will need to think first how they will protect themselves before they can do anything for another person.

That does not only apply when there is physical conflict or anger, but also in circumstances when male street pastors might be dealing with a lone female, or vice versa. On one occasion I met up with an all-male group of street pastors. After a tea break at about 12.30 a.m., we went back out on patrol, and the first incident we came across was a young lady whose drink had been spiked. As I observed the street pastors helping this woman, I was very encouraged by their textbook approach, important here because they were all men, dealing with a young woman. I was impressed that they put their training into practice. They found one of the girl's friends and brought her into the equation, so this tells me that they were thinking about their own safety as well as hers. They were able to make sure that both girls got into a taxi and went safely home.

Without love … with fear

It is important that street pastor volunteers understand the vacuum in society today. By this I mean that many people have an empty space in their lives where love should be. Many people can acutely feel this need to be loved and to have loved ones spend time with them, even if they can't or won't articulate their need. I strongly believe that the person who has the ability to give time and love to those who are vulnerable has the potential to soak up aggression. When someone is weighing whether to talk to us or not, whether to receive anything from us or not, what they are looking for is someone who will be available, someone who won't condemn them (but seek to understand them instead) and someone who can be of practical help to them.

> Exposes real issues in today's society.
>
> *Training evaluation, 'Youth Culture'*

> The strengths of the course are the complete openness and honesty about what to expect on the streets. It was great to hear the responses from business owners and nightclub workers towards the street pastors and to see the unity of church denominations involved in the scheme.
>
> *Training evaluation, 'Roles and Responsibilities'*

Fear for your own safety in the place where you live has been identified by the police as a key problem in our communities. Sadly many people live with fear as a part of their daily lives. The safety of our streets is something street pastors can influence. During training, trainees are encouraged to reflect on social cohesion. They are asked, 'What are the factors that produce cohesion? What are the factors that limit cohesion?' It is important for trainee street pastors to grapple with the big picture of the condition of our postmodern world—a culture that tells us that individuality is more important than belonging—and see the connections between this and the loneliness and fear in our communities.

> The first night I was out we saw a young woman throwing up next to a covered bin. I was touched by the way she

had tried to be tidy about it and also by the way the young man with her was holding her hair back for her as she bent over to heave.

I went up to them with a clean tissue that I held out as I asked if they could use a tissue. The young man looked at me suspiciously and said, 'How do I know there aren't drugs on that?' I was so shocked and saddened. I had no idea of the level of suspicion and fear with which our young people live.

Street pastor, Bridgend

I was with a group of street pastors in a London borough one night and we called in to speak to the owner of a newsagents shop. The man said he had been robbed at gunpoint the week before. He told us how when the gunman pulled the trigger, the gun jammed and the robber ran out. Naturally, the poor man was left with a deep sense of fear. He asked the street pastors to come back when he closed up the shop at 10.30 p.m. Two of the street pastors stood outside the shop, two stayed inside, and we all helped him to pull down the shutters, then escorted him with his takings into his car. It was a blessing to be able to support this man.

The man who owns the off-licence on the corner was so supportive of Street Pastors from the very beginning, always offering us food and drinks when we visited his shop on our patrol. A few of the street pastors formed a good friendship with him, so much so that he let us know of the problems he was having with football fans and youths as he closed the shop.

We were able to be there with him when he locked up at 11 p.m., helping him to feel safer. He also called us when his mother died. In this, we were able to pray for him and to support him in the difficult times that were to come.

Street pastor, Birmingham

I came to a nightclub one night where there were about fifty people all smoking outside the main entrance. Two young men in their early twenties asked me, 'What is a street pastor?' And so a conversation started. One of the lads began to tell me about the two scars that were very visible on his head. I asked how he had received them. He told me that two brothers had 'bottled him'. I responded to him as a father would respond to a son. I remember encouraging him—he was a bright articulate young man—to go back to college and pursue some formal education. Then I did something unusual: I offered to pray for him. Usually I wait for someone to ask me to pray for them. However, on this occasion I felt it was right to offer to pray there and then. Can you imagine the scene? There were loads of people around and lots of noise. As I prayed for the two young men I asked the Lord to encourage them, to heal the pain of those scars and their anger. One of the guys sighed when I had finished and said, 'I needed that. Thank you very much.'

CHAPTER THREE

SIMPLE BUT INNOVATIVE THINKING

Scottish Parliament, written answers, 22 January 2009

Local contexts: diversity and evaluation

We've had some real victories in certain areas where there has been a tough gang culture. We have seen our credibility grow in Moss Side, and now all the young people feel they can be confident that we won't break confidentiality because we're not the police. They respect our authority. One day myself and another street pastor were waiting for two Columbian pastors to meet us at the office in Moss Side. Time went by and eventually they called to say they couldn't get into the building. They said, 'We can't get up the street ... the police are everywhere.' We immediately came outside and saw pretty much what they had described. There were helicopters overhead, police vans everywhere and a massive crowd

of onlookers. We hurried over to the police cordons, told
them we were street pastors, and the officers opened
the barriers and let us through.

Incredibly, the sea of people parted, and after a while we
reached the source of the trouble. On the ground was a
half-naked man, handcuffed, with several police on top of
him. He was having an epileptic fit. An older man nearby
asked who we were and before we could say anything,
a kid answered, 'They're the street pastors.' Then other
kids took up the chant, 'They're the street pastors, they're
the street pastors.' Within five minutes the ambulance
had arrived, the man was taken to hospital and we hung
around talking to loads of people in the crowd.

It really showed me how much respect we had. The
authority of God was there. From that point on we began
to get to know the family of the young man (who eventually did get sentenced for armed robbery). In fact, before
he was imprisoned, the lad helped us with some research
on inner-city gangs. One day I called at his home, but he
wasn't in. I was with some friends, and as we left we
saw a large crowd of people farther down the road who
were very aggressive, shouting a lot. As we wondered
what to do, we happened to see the guy who we had
been looking for. We walked with him towards the trouble
and because all the young people knew and accepted
him, they accepted us too! We were able to say, 'C'mon

you'd better get off, or the police will be here.' They all dispersed in small groups. The police arrived later but didn't have to do anything. We see this happening a lot— the knock-on effects of our good reputation.

Street pastor, Inner South Manchester

Inner-city scenes such as this do not tell the whole story of Street Pastors. We are now seeing the initiative working in many different contexts around the country. The adaptability of the ethos has been a great eye-opener for me! Different environments present different challenges, but we can always start by asking the question, how do we interface with this community? Some urban contexts have what could be described as very 'obvious' antisocial behaviour and everyone agrees about what that behaviour is; in affluent suburban areas, a lack of community cohesion can be more discernible than specific problems of disorder or crime; in a village or a rural situation, the problems often centre around young people who have nothing to do. There may be no resources for them in the village and transport links to other places are poor. What do they do? They buy alcohol from the supermarket and get tanked up. Far from being redundant in these places, street pastors have realised that they can interact with those young people.

Many places are nice locations to visit during the day, and not generally thought of as troublespots, like the town of Perth in central Scotland.

People don't automatically think of Perth as being a rough place and it's quite nice during the day, but in certain areas it's not very nice at night. On the weekends it's thick with people in Mill Street and they're pouring out of the pubs across the road. In the nightclubs there is a lot of action.

Apart from that there are about four or five gangs in Perth, so it's not the quiet wee backwater that people might think.

Street pastor, Perth

Camborne in Cornwall is an ex-mining town with a population of 23,000 and the biggest conurbation in Cornwall. It has very little tourism, unlike the rest of the county, and is severely underfunded in terms of adult social services. Rural poverty is as devastating as poverty in the urban environment.

There is very little money for care in the community in the area, so a lot of what we do is about spending time with people, many of whom are lonely, many of whom are drug- and alcohol-dependent.

There are considerable social problems in the Camborne and Redruth area. In proportion to its population, it has a large amount of social housing. Over 50 percent of children live in one-parent families, over 50 percent of households are benefit-dependent, over 50 percent of adults have no qualifications, over 30 percent of people have no access to a car.[1]

---

1   Figures obtained from Cornwall County Council, 'Lower Super Output Area Profile', 2004.

> Street pastors in Camborne go out at night, but we also
> have an afternoon shift, a bit like School Pastors, but
> in our case, we operate out of the town square. There
> is a lot of street drinking, and we meet many homeless
> people and those suffering with mental health issues.
>
> *Street pastor, Camborne*

In places where the social problems are not as pervasive as some urban contexts, Street Pastors teams have met with the police and asked, 'What can you tell us about the problems in this area? What causes residents to be afraid? Are there particular hotspots where trouble starts? Are there particular times of day when your officers are under pressure?' We know that when Christians have asked the police, 'Where can we have a role?' they have built a foundation for engaging with their community, whatever the size or shape of that locality.

Out of that willingness to partner with the police and local authority has come many things. There may be one garage or shop that is the target of abuse or theft or vandalism. How can Street Pastors support and reassure its staff? Or the police may have a list of local families whose children are always in trouble. What kind of role can we have with them? Street pastors might be better received by those families because they are not social services or the police. Often, Street Pastors teams in small towns have told us that what might have taken months to build up in an urban context has taken only weeks in their area.

> We've made lots of contacts with people and have been
> able to form relationships with many because we see

the same people, and they see us, week in week out. We are very visible in a place the size of Heathfield. The whole town knows about Street Pastors, so you have to live the life, because everyone knows what is going on.

Street pastor, Heathfield

Heathfield is a small rural town right in the middle of East Sussex. Street pastors here are known as 'trustworthy friends of the community', a phrase first used by the rector of one of the churches in the town. Street pastors have found that the most productive time for them to be out is from 7.30 p.m., when they are able to meet lots of youngsters, and with only one pub, the town centre is quiet by about 11.30 p.m. In this context, street pastors have developed a good relationship with the primary school and the community college, taking assemblies and using the college as the venue for their commissioning service. Once a month street pastors do an afternoon shift, meeting school children and parents around the town. They have also taken the opportunity to have a presence at special town events like the carnival and the annual French market, which draws in thousands of visitors.

Whether urban or rural, there are always specific local issues for street pastors to respond to.

Sometimes trouble occurs in Torquay because of rivalries between Torquay people and other nearby towns. It does feel like a tribal place. When foreign students come, the problems are even more pronounced. The number of English language students is very high, and the police have put an officer in charge of relations with them. We are trying to develop our contacts with language schools, to make sure that information about Street Pastors is available to all students.

Street pastor, Torbay

School Pastors

When I was first exploring the idea and consulting with the police about the needs of the community, one of the most interesting statements I heard was that the time of day of greatest concern to them was 2 p.m. until 6 p.m. Between these hours young people leave school and make their way home. This daily occurrence produces a heightened level of fear or feelings of intimidation for some people, often residents whose homes are close to schools. Local traders often report incidents of fighting, shouting and stealing at the end of the school day. Many school children too find that the journey home from school presents an opportunity for bullying, harassment or theft.

As I was driving back to the office after a school visit one day, I noticed a group of young people. There seemed to be something strange about this group; a younger boy was in the middle of the group and one of the older ones was holding an iPod. I wondered if they had just 'jacked' (robbed) this young boy. I was in the middle of a three-lane road, but the traffic lights had just changed to red, so I wound my window down and called across to the group, 'What's happening? Are you jacking that guy?' Several of the boys shouted back that no, they weren't. I then called the boy himself over, and repeated my question, 'Are they jacking you?' Tears rolled down his cheeks, as he said, 'Yes, they are.'

I had the bus lane on my left, which I couldn't pull into because at that time of day I would get fined. The traffic lights were about to change to green. I turned off the engine, put my hazard lights on and took the keys out of the ignition. I had to think fast about how best to deal with this situation, and the blaring horns of the traffic behind my car did not help my concentration. My opening words to the group of lads were, 'Do you want to spend the rest of the day in a police cell? Do you want your mothers to come to the station and pick you up?' There was no response so I asked them again, 'Do you want your mothers to come and pick you up from a police cell?' Turning to the boy holding the iPod, I asked him to give it back. As they handed it over to the younger boy, I said to the group, 'You'd better go, because the police will be here any minute,' and they dispersed.

I became aware of other drivers shouting all kinds of things at me (it wasn't 'God bless you'), and I asked myself, 'How am I going to get this boy out of this area?' I couldn't leave him on his own, because the older guys might come looking for him. I couldn't give him a lift in my car for my own safety with regard to child protection issues. In the end I asked a lady at a nearby bus stop for help. 'Excuse me, madam,' I said, 'can you make sure this boy gets on the next bus?' She turned her head away. I couldn't believe it! However, at that point some of the boy's friends and their parents shouted to me from across the road. They had seen what had happened and were able to come over and take the boy home.

I have always felt that the roots of the disenfranchisement experienced by many young men and women who are on the margins of society may well go back into their early teenage years, or even earlier. I know that the gang culture exists among this age group, sometimes based on common interests or geography. Many teenagers feel unsafe by themselves and hence move about in large groups for a sense of safety. There is also a considerable problem of theft among children and teenagers, particularly of mobile phones.

I once received a call from the headteacher of a school in Southeast London, who informed me that one of his students had turned up at school with a bulletproof vest on. I was asked to come to the school immediately, so I left what I was doing and went. When I arrived I was taken to meet the boy, and I began to listen to his story. Several times he told me that he didn't 'give a damn' about life. He told me how his father had promised never to leave him, but one day he had. 'Nobody gives a damn about me, and I don't give a damn about life,' he repeated. He was wearing the bulletproof vest because he had disrespected a member of a gang that operated in the postcode of the school, and he knew he was in line for a retaliation attack. As he was happy to risk his own life, he was determined to face this gang and attempt to kill one of them first.

In agreement with the boy's mother and his school, I responded by offering to pick him up from school every day for a few weeks so that he was not so vulnerable. I also asked if I could meet his parents. Not long after this I met his mother in person and was able to listen to her story.

She'd had a breakdown; her eldest son was on drugs, her daughter was getting mixed up with the wrong crowd and she couldn't cope with her youngest son, the one I had met. His mother felt it was best to send the boy to live with relatives abroad, and when this happened, I kept in contact with the teenager. A year later when he returned I met up with him, and I'm delighted that he is now going to college.

This story has had a happy ending, but there are many that don't. Many young people are so disappointed with life, they can't see the point of holding onto anything, their own life included.

Fear of knife crime among teenagers is so high in some places that school children have to walk through metal detectors before boarding the school bus. This strategy—an attempt to reassure children and parents—was used in Purley, Surrey, in the summer of 2008, as part of Operation Blunt, led by the Safer Neighbourhood Ward Panel.[2]

Alongside this initiative, Ascension Trust piloted a School Pastors scheme in Purley in 2008[3]. Six school pastors met youngsters at Thomas More Catholic School in the town, and walked with them to the bus stop. They then waited with the young people and split into pairs to travel with the youngsters on the three different buses that take them to Croydon. After two months of having school pastors available to them, children at the school went to their headteacher and said that they preferred to go home on a bus where there was a school pastor, rather than on one where there was not.

Purley Baptist Church's associate minister, Pam Bryan, describes local pupils as usually well-behaved but often intimidating when they are in a crowd.[4]

---

2   *Croydon Advertiser*, 4 July 2008.

3   The work of Ascension Trust is described more fully in chapter 4.

4   *Croydon Advertiser*, 27 February 2009.

> There's a lot of exuberance from a lot of pretty decent
> kids arriving all at one time in a community that's got
> quite a lot of older people. If we can help them draw
> the line between exuberance and misbehaviour, then the
> majority of us are better off.

Many kids won't go upstairs on the bus because they are more likely to be robbed or beaten up on the upper deck. If children feel vulnerable, there is an adult there who is available to listen and care. A school pastor's role is to be part of a protective 'umbrella' for children and youth, and to build good relationships with local shopkeepers, the local police and responsible people at bus and train stations where young people congregate.[5] Our pilot scheme, launched in Purley at the request of the Home Office, indicates that our partners in government and local government are now shaping the diversification of the Street Pastors model. We have now been asked to roll out this initiative in schools across London, and there is much interest around the country.

How are we doing?

Independent evaluation produces a variety of evidence that is useful in determining the efficacy of Street Pastors and in building a picture of the ways in which different teams have fitted into different statutory partnerships in response to different local needs. Independent evaluation is primarily useful in three ways: for outside agencies who want to know whether we are effective or not; for ourselves, to give

---

5   Training in the following areas, in addition to the Street Pastors training, is required for a school pastor: relating to adolescents, understanding the secondary school system, peer pressure, Youth Services (Social Services), young people and the law.

us authority when we speak to people about Street Pastors and seek
to develop our partnerships; and to answer our *own* questions about
how effective we are.[6]

We should not shy away from evaluation because through it we
can learn a good deal about our practices. Experience has shown me
that a Christian's sense of responsibility for society, politics or culture
is often subject to the filter of political correctness, prejudice, the
dictates of tolerance or the charge of exclusivity. For this reason, I
sometimes feel that the evaluation process needs to be prefaced by
the statement, 'We are Christians; please accept us as such.' Nobody
should expect us to be any more than we are, but we want everyone to understand that we are informed people, socially conscious
people, and our religion challenges us to be relevant.

To date, Street Pastors in Southwark, Plymouth, Manchester
and Portsmouth have been scrutinised in independent evaluations.
In some cases, like that of Street Pastors in Southwark, evaluation
like this has been the route to secure funding. An independent
company was charged with the task of evaluation because Southwark
Council was considering funding our teams in Peckham and
Camberwell, and they wanted to establish what kind of risk they
would be taking.[7] They interviewed us, came out with us at night,
and looked at our organisational structure. The report, prepared
in the first six months of our work in the borough, looks at the
strengths and weaknesses of Street Pastors and the crime statistics for

---

6   Alternatively, 'in-house' evaluation is carried out on a weekly basis by street pastors themselves, often in the form of a diary
    or record sheet, which is then available for use by a coordinator and/or police. Annual reviews are useful for identifying issues
    that need development. Collection of data by the Street Pastors team themselves, or a 'performance brief' issued by local
    police, can help to establish the annual impact of the service and can be used to communicate to partner agencies and
    secure sustainable funding.

7   The report is dated October 2005.

hotspots in the area. It noted the success that street pastors were having in reducing crime and disorder on the streets and, in particular, affirmed their nonjudgmental approach.

The area analysed to produce the statistics for criminal behaviour in the report stretches from Rye Lane in Peckham, along Camberwell Church Street, and into Peckham Road (the area where Damilola Taylor was killed). Street pastors regularly walk that mile. Many robberies happen in that area, but street pastors have prevented numerous incidents by their presence. How do I know that? Because, in comparative figures for the thirteen-week period October to January 2003–4 and 2004–5 (before and after Street Pastors began operating), the evaluation shows that serious disorder offences reduced on average by 95 percent in the Peckham patrol area, and by 74 percent in the Camberwell patrol area.

In some areas, independent evaluation has been a key part of progress. For Manchester South Street Pastors, their evaluation by Manchester City Council's Crime and Disorder Unit means that they will be able to take their place as one of the very few voluntary organisations involved in the crime and disorder partnership. The report was produced after a policy officer from the unit shadowed the team. Now, when the statutory bodies meet together to identify areas of crime in the city and ways of addressing it, Street Pastors is one of the resources available to be part of the response. The team may be tasked, for example, with building relationships with a particular family or individual.

The evaluation of Street Pastors in Plymouth by academics at the University of Plymouth has been produced in conjunction with the police, and has largely been paid for by the Community Safety partnership. In this case, analysis was instigated by ourselves and the coordinator of the teams in Plymouth, because we both wanted to know how we were doing in that area. The local authority is working with very tight budgets in Plymouth and has not been forthcoming in terms of supporting Street Pastors. So we hope that when the evaluation is presented to the council it will add weight to our case.[8]

> Plymouth is not South London. We have a community made up of 30,000 students, naval families, many servicemen who are looking to let off steam, and poorly paid locals who feel that they are discriminated against economically. There is a gradual rise in ethnic minorities and we now have two mosques in the city. The students are mostly good-natured; they drink a lot, but they don't get too aggressive. When we go into the naval areas, the atmosphere is far less friendly. There is more drinking, aggression, violence, less frivolity and a high police concentration. We can be up to our ears in vomit, blood, anger, depression, serious drunkenness, hardship and homelessness.
>
> *Street pastor, Plymouth*

Portsmouth Street Pastors have been evaluated by a Public Health Practitioner trainee in research initiated by Portsmouth City Primary Care Trust.[9] Street Pastors began operating in Portsmouth

---

8   At the time of writing, the final copy of the evaluation of Street Pastors in Plymouth was not ready for release.

9   With resources provided by South Central Health Authority via the Public Health Practitioner Training Scheme. The report is written by Peter Cornish, with the cooperation of Portsmouth Street Pastors and Elly Mulvany, coordinator.

in June 2007, and with the support of Local Strategic Partnerships (LSPs), they are now an integral part of 'Operation Drink Safe', a local alcohol harm management campaign that has been introduced in Portsmouth alongside other key initiatives such as the Alcohol Interventions Team and Taxi Marshalls. This teamwork approach to the high levels of alcohol-related violence on the streets of the city includes measures to control the use of alcohol and deal with the problems of related crime and disorder. It has seen a 62 percent reduction in alcohol-fuelled violence against the person in the period July 2007–8, compared to the previous twelve months. The report acknowledges Street Pastors' contribution to this improvement and concludes that street pastors are good at making contact with people on the street, calming aggressive behaviour and building strong relationships with partners in the night time economy. It notes the positive public perception of the team and the effect street pastors have had in reducing the fear of crime.[10]

The Home Office

The Home Office is always looking out for creative initiatives. In the early years of Street Pastors, it was in a similar position to the police: the Home Office had heard things about us but didn't know how much substance we had. Ascension Trust first came into contact with the Home Office at the time of our discussions with the police about the weapons and drugs protocol agreement. Officials from the Home Office were involved in those meetings. From our first meeting it

---

10 The report also interviews people on the streets, providing a breakdown of the ages of contacts made by street pastors, the numbers of respondents who have/have not heard of Street Pastors, and the percentage of respondents who believe that street pastors made the area safer.

was obvious that it was important for us to communicate effectively about the church in this country, as the denominational complexity of the church and its potential in terms of a national network was unfamiliar to them. Their support was critical—even when our dealings with them were largely about risk assessment and operating procedures—because we were already thinking that the agreements we made with the police needed to be applicable to the whole country: the Home Office and the police would be able to help us push it further afield.[11]

I believe that the Home Office liked what we were doing because it was well thought through, and there was a clear process and accountability. I know that they still don't fully understand the church picture, but they like the results we get and the fact that we are passionate about what we do. They know that we are practitioners on the ground, and this experience makes us useful to policy making.

For example, in the past we have been invited to meetings with David Blunkett, then home secretary, to discuss knife crime. He wanted to hear from us what was happening and what should be done in terms of intervention. At other times we have been a sounding board when a policy is being launched. This kind of dialogue goes on several times a year.[12] Policy makers can collect data but they are not out on the streets at the times of the night that we are, and so they need us to talk to them because we have that experience on the ground. There are strategic partnerships like this between government and grassroots organisations up and down the country.

---

11 See chapter 7 for these discussions.

12 For instance, Ascension Trust submitted written evidence to the Home Affairs Committee in the Session 2006–7, as part of an inquiry into public perceptions of young black people and the criminal justice system.

One example would be the Safer Neighbourhood Teams, who work in partnership with local agencies to address public concerns about antisocial and nuisance behaviour.

Our partnership with the Home Office has enabled us to use the Home Office logo, which gives a stamp of respectability and credibility. The Home Office hasn't put a lot of money into Street Pastors but it has given us the money to develop our training manual. The Office is also talking to us about the possibility of developing School Pastors. I feel that we have helped the Home Office to see that churches are part of the fabric of every community. Jacqui Smith MP has said that she would like to see street pastors on every street in this country. Speaking at a crackdown on gangs in Birmingham, the minister praised the job that street pastors do.[13]

> They are not soft, these people. They are community representatives whom people trust and can intervene to stop youngsters from going down that road [into gangs].
>
> *Jacqui Smith, former home secretary*

We have enjoyed the company of several Home Office ministers who have wanted to get a better idea of what we are doing and the problems that communities face. MPs Vernon Coaker and Tony McNulty visited our office and went out with a group of street pastors one Friday night in 2007.[14]

---

13 *Daily Mirror*, 11 March 2008.

14 In 2007 Vernon Coaker was undersecretary of state in the Home Office. Tony McNulty took over a portfolio for policing and crime in May 2006.

After a short prayer time we got into a discussion with the two men about the high proportion of female street pastors and their effectiveness. Before long it was time to get going and we made our way through the estate, the MPs wearing Street Pastors 'Observer' jackets. In the distance we could see that there was some disturbance among a large group of youths. On seeing this, a few of the street pastors and the two MPs stayed on the other side of the road, and some of the others went over to see if they could bring calm to this volatile situation. One of the street pastors that night was Edith, a woman with a massive heart for her community. We watched as she went up to the tallest and most agitated youth in the group. Going into 'mumsy' mode, she grabbed him by the hand and gently tugged him away from the group. On seeing this, Vernon Coaker said, 'My gosh, that's brave!' Eustace replied to him, 'No, if you or I had approached that youth, it would have been brave!' By which he meant that Edith (like many women street pastors) had a tremendous rapport with young people and could quickly soften a tense situation. That was exactly what we saw happen that night. As the young man realised it was 'nan' he was dealing with, his body language changed and visibly relaxed. Edith talked to him for ten minutes and at no point did he attempt to remove his hand from hers.

The group dispersed without any trouble. We walked some of the youths to safety in the direction that we were going. The story went that the dispute had started when one guy had had his saveloy sausage knocked out of his portion of chips, and felt he had been disrespected. Later that evening somebody came up to us and asked, 'What is a street pastor?' It was Mr McNulty who answered the question—quite comprehensively!

Fiona Mactaggart, who was at the time a Home Office minister with responsibility for the criminal justice system, also came out with us in Peckham. One of the first things she said to me was that she was an atheist. I said I didn't mind what she was, as long as we could solve some problems on the streets. She spent two hours with us. She was surprised at the number of gangs she saw in operation the night she was out and the ease with which we interacted with them. We drew alongside a group of boys in Camberwell and got talking to an eighteen-year-old who had done his 'A' levels but didn't have a job. The minister was amazed that standing before her was a bright young guy who could speak for forty minutes about how hopeless things were for him. He didn't know who she was, but no doubt she walked away that night knowing that successive governments were failing to reach some people.

In Hastings the initiative behind Street Pastors came from the local MP, Michael Foster, Member for Hastings and Rye. I had met him at a prayer breakfast, and soon afterwards received a letter from the MP saying that he planned to assess support for Street Pastors in his area and invite church leaders from the town to a breakfast meeting to discuss the subject. Street Pastors in Hastings is now up and running. The opportunity to speak at the speaker's private residence in the Palace of Westminster was given to me by Jim Dobbin, MP for Heywood and Middleton, Greater Manchester. At this event in 2008 I was able to meet cross-party MPs and challenge them to have conviction like Wilberforce and Shaftesbury. 'Come and hang out with us,' I said, and several MPs have done just that, spending an evening with their local Street Pastors team, walking the streets.

Good practice

One year after the protocol agreement with the police had been completed, we met Home Office officials again and were able to tell them that Street Pastors were now working in Birmingham and Manchester. They were really surprised! The next time that we met with them they were taken aback that we were no longer talking simply about major cities but about areas like Southend, Kingston and Wrexham. As one senior civil servant put it, 'We didn't realise that you guys would go so far!' When they came to the annual Street Pastors dinner in 2005 they were equally surprised to find that they were having dinner with another four hundred guests! They began to realise that this wasn't just a project that was based in Brixton but that it reflected the national church, and there were no boundaries to culture or colour. The geographical spread of the initiative has been a significant factor in the informal and formal evaluation of Street Pastors, and it has helped many people to take us seriously.

Street Pastors is now operating in many different areas of the country, and we recognise that, because antisocial behaviour is a problem in a small rural town as well as the inner city, there is a need for the Street Pastors model to be flexible enough for teams to develop the initiative to meet their local needs, whether that be in an urban, suburban, coastal or rural context. In this way the initiative will help the widest possible group of churches and Christians to have a Christian presence in their communities. We provide the framework for a Street Pastors team and present to them the parameters they should operate within to ensure quality, but if that team finds that they are tailoring good practices to their local needs, that is great. More than this, we encourage coordinators to feed these developments in to us, so that we can incorporate them into the delivery of the initiative to other cities and towns. We need to pioneer good practices and draw in advice from other organisations so that we can stay sharp and be as effective as possible.

For one coordinator, 'Good practice is being willing to tell anybody and everybody about Street Pastors!'[15] For some teams, good practice is adapting or adding elements to the training programme in response to local needs. For others, it may be an emphasis on creative publicity, such as advertising Street Pastors on beer mats, together with the information about the route that they walk and the mobile phone number for the team. In Manchester, ex-gang members and ex-drug dealers have been brought into training sessions in order for Street Pastors trainees to learn firsthand about those lifestyles, in particular why there is so much 'respect' among young people for them. Other teams have found a need to have training from Cruse Bereavement Care and the Samaritans because they have come across many people who are grieving for loved ones. Good practice is gleaning relevant information or skills to support trainees to respond to the needs that they come across on the street.

As reported widely in the press, the distribution of flip-flops to young women who have taken off their high-fashion shoes and are at risk of injuring their feet has been a simple and effective action at the point of need. Some teams also give out free 'spikeys', a small plastic

---

15 I am grateful to Ros and Roger Ede for conversations about good practice in the context of this chapter.

stopper that goes in the neck of a bottle through which a straw can be inserted, thus protecting that drink from being contaminated or 'spiked'. This has enabled Street Pastors teams to improve their contact with young women, a group that some have found to be initially less responsive than men to the presence of street pastors. As they give them out, they can say, 'Take this, keep yourself safe—we will be here for you later if you need us.'

Other areas have placed great importance on media training courses for their senior street pastors, in order to make sure that these representatives know how to speak to the press. In South Manchester, Street Pastors' relationship with university students is one of the key characteristics of the initiative as it has developed in that area. When students want to include Street Pastors in their thesis—whether they are researching crime and the justice system, media relations or the role of the church in the lives of young people—trained street pastors collaborate with them to provide information. The team in South Manchester have also had input into a large research project for Manchester University on inner-city gangs, and have introduced researchers to gang members. For this team, the opportunity to represent the work of Street Pastors in research that will influence the way people think in years to come is another dimension of good practice.

Street Pastors in Manchester have also worked in partnership with the police as part of Operation Cougar, designed to take violent gangs and their guns off the streets. Like all Street Pastors teams they are independent of the police, but senior street pastors and coordinators in this locality have been proactive in tackling crime and gangs, working with communities, making sure that information flows freely within them. They have been part of Home Office evaluations of community initiatives and place a priority on feeding back information about which government initiatives are working and why, and what is successful for community and police relations.

CHAPTER FOUR

HOW THE MEN IN CASSOCKS BECAME THE BOYS IN THE HOOD

The Times, 5 July 2003

The birth of Street Pastors

In 1992 I was a church leader in London, fresh from a two-week mission in Wolverhampton that had taken place under the Churches Together banner. What I had seen going on in that city made an impression on me. I had been paired with a church in the city led by an Anglican minister, Alistair Palmer, a man who was in the process of reorienting his ministry in response to the call of the Lord to look outwards into his community as well as pastor his congregation. One of the things he was doing was setting up a refuge for drug addicts. During my stay in Wolverhampton I had also met a group of nuns who had relocated from their convent onto a council estate in order to serve the people there. Through these two acts of service and outreach, God spoke to me profoundly, not just about my ministry but about the ministry of the church in Britain as a whole.

Although I was already taking the message of Jesus to many different locations in the community, I began to realise that I was staying comfortably within the conventions of church mission. It gradually dawned on me that the formula for church mission, as I knew it, went something like this: allow two years to plan for a mission, deliver the mission over a two-week period, take a further two years to recover from the mission, and add on another two years of evaluation to decide whether it should be done again. As I found myself thinking like this, dissatisfaction grew in me, and I was led to reflect on the whole concept and culture of church mission. I realised that, whereas the church was providing short bursts of outreach activity, what people were looking for in their communities was consistency and continuity.

Not long after that mission, Alistair Palmer got in touch with me to tell me that two friends of his, ministers from the Episcopalian Church in Pennsylvania in the United States, were visiting Britain. He asked if I would entertain them for a weekend, and mentioned that they had interesting stories to tell about drugs, guns and gangs in the States. Having been in a gang as a teenager, I was very curious to meet them and to hear of their experience and insight.

When they arrived at my house, we wasted no time in getting into conversation about these issues. I remember quite clearly asking them what response they had met with from the British church with regard to these social problems. In their opinion, came the reply, the church was very much detached from them. On closer questioning, it transpired that part of the plan for their visit was also to hold meetings with the police and local government officers in various locations around the country. Again, I asked, 'What response did you receive?' The police, they told me, had thanked them for their trouble, but had reassured the two visitors that the activities they had described were an American problem. Local councils, the pastors reported, had been as complacent as the police. 'We don't have that kind of problem here,' they had said.

During these conversations, the Pennsylvanian pastors made plain to me the devastation caused to communities by the problems of guns and drugs and the high level of violence associated with these activities. They had talked of the massive amounts of money made by drug dealing. I didn't know what to do with this information. What I didn't realise at the time was that God was saying to me that He would use me to respond to what I was hearing. I suppose my experience was a bit like Mary's—she was able to receive the news from the angel about the birth of Jesus even when it made no sense to her (Luke 1:34–38)! The two men from Pennsylvania had told me of things that were happening thousands of miles away in a different culture. And I, like the police and the local councils, couldn't truly relate them to our situation in this country.

Moving forward some five years, those same conversations came back to me quite forcefully when Ascension Trust, the charitable organisation of which I was the director, began to receive phone calls from the press requesting statements about the reasons for increasing levels of crime and violence in our communities. The Cullen Inquiry of 1996, which followed the Dunblane Massacre, had drawn a link between gun ownership and crime and recommended tighter control of handgun ownership, and there was much public and political inter-est in the subject, with gun amnesties planned for the anniversary of the shootings at Dunblane.[1] The Firearms Amendment Act was passed by Tony Blair's newly elected government in 1997.

'Boy hurt in gang attack', *The Sunday Times*, 02.02.97

'Highest rise in violent crime for seven years', *The Times*, 18.03.97

'Every gun should be outlawed', *The Sun*, 30.04.97

'Britain could be facing crime crisis', *The Times*, 13.06.97

'Five held following 400-gun haul', *The Independent*, 18.07.97

'Young are committing 13 crimes each minute', *The Times*, 26.07.97

'Youth gang linked to murder, rape and street attacks', *The Times*, 17.12.97

Since its inception in 1993, Ascension Trust had been training local churches in urban and cross-cultural mission, helping them to look at some of the social issues that had to be addressed if churches were going to be effective in outreach. We were working at a

---

1 In March 1996, sixteen children and one teacher were shot dead at the primary school in Dunblane, Scotland.

grassroots level and understood the makeup, the DNA if you like, of the issues that were troubling communities. Journalists were asking us how the church was going to respond. They wanted to know what we thought the government should be doing.

I founded Ascension Trust in 1993 out of my concern to see churches involved in mission relevant to their own context and locality. From the outset I was particularly concerned about the small numbers of ethnic minorities in full-time ministry across the denominations, and so the Trust was set up to work with local churches and theological colleges to explore the subject of urban mission. At first it primarily targeted African and Caribbean churches, though not exclusively. The Trust's focus was on training individuals and churches for social action and sharing the gospel in ways that were relevant to the needs of their communities.

The other arm of Ascension Trust's remit was to work with young people, exposing them to different church contexts and helping them to lead social action projects. This took place around Britain and Europe, and later in the United States and South America. I wanted to encourage Christians to have a global perspective on mission and a desire to serve other countries with skills and expertise.

As a Christian I was used to people asking about salvation, but I was a lot less ready for questions about my practical response to social and cultural issues. I started to ask myself what the Bible says about a Christian's response to society. What does the Bible teach? How do I implement my response in a real, practical and physical way? The Bible tells me that Jesus came from heaven but lived on this earth. He actually fed people (Matt. 14:15–21); He helped Peter pay his taxes (Matt. 17:27); and He stood up for those who were poor and marginalised.

This says to me that Jesus was very practical. The fact that He was always walking around and engaging with people shows me that it was very much part of His ministry to meet people's needs where they were.

As I read the Bible and sought to interpret it, the challenge for me was to take Scripture seriously and to work out what effect it should have on my day-to-day life. I asked myself, what were the things I needed to do to show that Jesus still loves, Jesus still cares and Jesus still provides a way through difficult situations? Many things can be worked out satisfactorily in theology, but what was the use of that if I didn't know how to apply the Bible to real, twenty-first-century life? At the same time as I formed these questions, I knew there was another equally big challenge awaiting me: how would I translate my own embryonic thoughts and understanding into the ability to convince other people to do something about these issues too?

Trends

By this time in 1997 my radar was active, and I began to pick up more accounts of violence, particularly in urban contexts and among the Caribbean community. Recalling the words of the two American pastors five years earlier, I began to realise that once these problems begin to manifest themselves, they just keep growing. Though they might start in an urban community, the impact would always be felt more widely.

Growing up in the inner city as I had done, I knew firsthand that my generation—the children of the first Caribbean immigrants—had experienced particular social conditions in the 1960s that were now starting to have repercussions on a big scale. In the sixties there had been a massive culture clash between West Indian culture and

British culture; we experienced a lack of opportunity in education, poor housing and conflict with the police. Deprivation, family breakdown, a sense of hopelessness, absent fathers and the lack of parental guidance were also part of the picture. Plus, you didn't need to be a mathematician to see the tremendous growth in money-making opportunities. Whereas, as a fifteen-year-old, I had sold a wrap of ganja for a handful of loose change, hundreds of pounds could be made selling the drugs that were now available. The activities I had been involved in—gangs, violence and drugs—were still at the hub of the problems, but the stakes were now much higher. In terms of drugs, accessibility to money was easier. Big money was involved. A fourteen-year-old could make £2,000 in a week as a runner, taking drugs from one place to another. Dealers, of course, could make much more. Accessibility to alcohol was also much greater. On top of this, the cycles of poverty and deprivation (social and emotional) that were part of the landscape of 1960s urban Britain were still turning. Family breakdown was greater, and opportunities for good jobs were still limited.

I approached my board of trustees with the message that the church needed to respond to the issues of drugs, guns and gangs. The Trust was ideally placed to respond. We had the necessary contacts with churches, and headed by myself, a black Caribbean leader, we understood the dynamics of an issue that was largely, if not exclusively, focused on the Caribbean community. The needs of our nation seemed so great that we felt it was important to give our time and attention to what was happening at home.

As I gathered my thoughts and painted this picture to the trustees, I was looking not just at drugs or guns or gangs, but at trends in the wider society. I felt strongly that it was right to link a shooting incident to the breakdown of our communities. Yes, it was totally appropriate to talk about street fights between gangs in the same breath as the change in people's value systems. People were no longer accountable to each other; there was more mobility—you didn't know everyone in your street anymore, whereas once this would have been the norm; antisocial behaviour was fast on the increase; there were older people who were barricading their doors with furniture because they were fearful of break-ins during the night. There was an increase in firearm incidents and a rising death rate associated with these incidents.

All these things made me sit up and take notice. The conclusion that I reached with the trustees at that time was that we needed to get an up-to-date picture of the situation and the response that was needed. As an organisation, we began an exercise of consultation and analysis to find some answers. Now, sixteen years after its creation, Ascension Trust is almost wholly focused on administering Street Pastors, with about 5 percent of its time spent on training and mission. Like my own calling, Ascension Trust's ministry has also evolved and, as the governing body of the Street Pastors initiative, it is now legally responsible for Street Pastors.

Heaven and hell coexist

A significant part of the information-gathering process was my visit to Jamaica. This formative relationship began in 2000 when a pastor from Jamaica, Bobby Wilmot, visited England and asked for a meeting with me. He said he had read my first book, *Dreadlocks*, and much of what I had communicated in that book was what he was experiencing in Kingston, but on a far greater scale. He began to share with me some of his experiences.

Bobby was the pastor of Covenant Community Church in Trench Town, a deprived area of Kingston, which, in alliance with a group of churches from the 'uptown' part of the city, was developing training and job schemes, and had set up a school in Rema, Trench Town. Lorna Stanley, the founder of Operation Restoration and headmistress of the school, had demonstrated extraordinary commitment to serve that ravaged community and its violent and depraved young people.[2] The uptown churches, led by Bruce Fletcher, had done some social analysis of the issues and their chief causes. When they started their work, people didn't trust them; they assumed they just wanted to convert them. Gradually, however, they opened up to them, and Bobby, Lorna and others found that they were able to begin to negotiate with people in ways that could help them break out of their lifestyle.

The following year I visited Jamaica together with a trustee of Ascension Trust, Jimi Adeleye. Jamaica is one of the most beautiful countries on this planet, but warped by great extremes of wealth and poverty, beauty and desperation. As you approach the island by air, you can see the mansions and mountains of the prestigious Beverly Hills area, with all the luxuries and opportunities that life affords. Yet only a ten-minute drive from there are some of the most deprived neighbourhoods. Pastor Bobby told me that Jamaica had a higher church attendance than any other country in the world, but for a small nation it also had an extremely high homicide rate. I felt the Lord saying to me that here heaven and hell coexist.

---

2   To read interviews with Lorna Stanley, or find out more about Operation Restoration, see www.jamaicans.com and www.news.bbc.co.uk/1/hi/programmes/crossing continents.

Bobby guided me around Trench Town. As I entered Collie Smith Drive, I was reminded of the images I had seen on television of war-torn Kosovo. Shelled-out buildings were everywhere. I was horrified to discover that the army had a strong presence in the area because the local constabulary could not keep the high incidence of gun crime under control. For the first time I wondered if I had done the right thing. Was my insurance policy up to date? Would I come out of this place alive? The reality and intensity of aggression really hit me as I entered that place. We negotiated our way around fridges, burnt-out cars and other large objects that had been deliberately left in the road to make it harder for gunmen in cars to drive straight down the street shooting. I saw policemen and soldiers patrolling in open-top jeeps, carrying high-powered rifles and machine guns.

On arrival at the school in Rema, I met young children who were really enjoying education. As I spoke with the teachers, they told me of some of the challenges they faced. Many of these kids only had a mother at home, they often had brothers and sisters from different fathers, and their mothers hadn't completed their own education. There was a small fee for the child to attend the school, but the teachers found that this money was often spent on a new outfit for the mother instead of on the child's schooling. Many times the school would just have to waive the fees.

Listening to Lorna, I heard how her greatest challenge was the older children, the nine- ten- and eleven-year-olds, who were very often already being groomed to be gang members and use guns. Gangs were all around these children—uncles and brothers were in the gang, their mother's boyfriend was in it. It was impossible to live in that community without being affected by gangs. Saddest of all, the majority of people in that neighbourhood had over the years had a member of their family murdered by gangs. Attending funerals was a regular event for everyone.

After I had been at the school for a few hours, Bobby suggested we take a walk. Would I be safe away from the school grounds? I wondered. But as we walked, I realised the high level of respect that there was among the young gunmen for Pastor Bobby and Miss Lorna and what they were doing at the school. I remember a young man who was standing at the corner of the street. Bobby asked him how he was. He replied, 'I'm bleached out.' I later found that this meant that he had been up all night, because he had been standing on the street corner as a lookout, watching for other gangs who might attack. He had to stay on guard to make sure his territory was safe at night.

'I hope you are not going to be firing guns around here today,' Pastor Bobby said to him. The young man replied, 'No, pastor, I have buried my gun.'

Immediately I thought, why didn't Pastor Bobby ask him to give up his gun? Pastor Bobby explained to me that if the lookout had handed in his gun, he would have been defenceless, and very likely have been killed. His gun was a deterrent to stop others attacking. Each day gang members made decisions about whether they carried a gun or not. If they did, they ran the risk of being caught when the police or soldiers raided, and might then face imprisonment. If they didn't, they made themselves an easy target for rival gangs.

I was equally taken aback by the high level of respect that the young man in Trench Town—probably a killer—had for Pastor Bobby. Bobby Wilmot had learnt how to be relevant; he had the ability to communicate with gunmen and develop relationships so that people trusted him. He was willing to relate to them, physically, in their context.

A council of war

After we had walked around the area, I was taken to a ministers' fraternal meeting. I will never forget how different this meeting was from any other ministers' meeting I had attended. In London, meetings like this were about how big your church was, whether your offering was up or down, the repairs that might be needed for your building or perhaps theological questions—did you agree with this or that practice? We ate sandwiches, prayed a bit and then went home. In this meeting, however, from start to finish, they talked about who was murdered last week, whose funeral they would be leading, how they would support each other, who had been told to leave the community by gunmen and how they should respond. I sat and listened to the story of a mother of forty-two years of age, with two sons, one of whom had killed someone. Gang members had said she was 'a bad influence' and had given her a date and time by which she was to leave the community. She was defiant, stayed in her home, and was killed when that deadline had passed.

The pastors talked about how they would meet at a victim's house to pray, wearing white T-shirts so that they would be recognised as pastors (a gathering crowd would otherwise be viewed very suspiciously). What hit me was that these ministers recognised that they had to get over differences in tradition and theology—issues related to how they did 'church'. They knew that unless they united they wouldn't make any impact on the problems. I remember thinking it felt like a council of war! Everything in that meeting was about death and vulnerability. Yet each one of those church leaders represented hope, because they spoke about what they were going to do together. They had ideas about education, training, employment, rehabilitation; about counselling people and helping those who had experienced nothing but violence. These church ministers knew that they were in a dire situation, but they had hope.

I, however, left that meeting with as much fear as hope. Could our streets at home get this bad? Again, I was aware that my response was two-fold, and contradictory: first, my experience of the pain, suffering and hopelessness of many of the people in these communities left me feeling that there was nothing good there. Second, by contrast, I felt that the best of everything was there. Jamaica has a good educational system; Jamaicans have generated wealth and have contributed not just to that region but internationally. I have returned to Jamaica every year since 2001, and every time I have been there, I have undoubtedly been inspired by the tenacity of people who have a heart to see the back of these problems, from the governor general to police officers to government ministers and church leaders.

It was during my first visit, however, that I discovered the complexity of the arguments surrounding the carrying of weapons. Like the lookout I had been introduced to by Pastor Bobby in Rema, young men carried weapons not just to attack, but to deter attacks from happening. Later I heard the same arguments used by young people in London to justify their possession of a gun, knife or metal bar. It is because of these complexities that those of us who wish to help cannot make simple interventions. Individuals involved in gun crime say that they don't trust the police: they feel there is no justice for them, and that they exist in a world apart from the courts and legal system that the rest of us rely on. They have their own rules. Taking away weapons makes those people very vulnerable.

> Research ... on gang development in Waltham Forest has cast further light on the ages of those becoming involved in gang activity ... gang development could be seen as an extension of younger bullying networks that vulnerable young people were required to negotiate in their communities. For some, joining the gang, albeit reluctantly, was preferable to being victimised by it ... Such findings seem entirely consistent with the work of ethnographic researchers ... detailing how young males in particular are required to negotiate their masculinity and 'street cred' in impoverished, oppressive and often highly competitive environments.
>
> *'Gun Crime: a review of evidence and policy' (2008)*
> *Centre for Crime and Justice, Kings College, London*

Knowing the challenge in Jamaica, I said to myself, the church in the UK must act before we reach anything like the scale of problems there. As I flew back to England, I was asking myself how church leaders would respond to what I was going to share with them. What effect would it have on my role as a local pastor? Where would I find the time to take on this vast issue of drugs, guns and gangs?

Guns on our streets
All these things had awakened my attention—the pastors from Pennsylvania, my experience in Jamaica and the growth in crime

levels in the UK—and by 2002 I was beginning to understand drugs, guns and gangs as the tip of an iceberg, with a cocktail of various antisocial behaviours lurking beneath the waterline. Intimidation, joyriding, carjacking, vandalism, drunkenness and violence are all serious offences in themselves, but perhaps the most serious thing about antisocial behaviour like this is that it escalates. Another factor that I felt would drive street crime to another level was fear. Fear is a great enemy because it touches many, many people—those with no connection to drugs or gun crime as well as those who are involved in it.

I believed the situation was getting worse and started to see that Ascension Trust, like any other lone voice, was going to come up against indifference and complacency. The church, the police and government agencies were insisting that there were only isolated incidents in pockets of our urban scene, which, they believed, could be contained and curbed. This drove me to the point where I knew I had to give up the leadership of my church in South London in order to sound the warning bell and get church leaders on board to do something about it.

I shared with my fellow leaders in Ichthus Christian Fellowship, and some months later, after bringing the issue up again, it was agreed that Ichthus would get behind me, and I would invite Pastors Bobby Wilmot and Bruce Fletcher to talk with church leaders and community leaders in London about the realities of drugs, guns and gangs. The challenge was to raise the finances to make the visit possible, and then to make the participants and the discussion mobile, so that we would be, in effect, a roadshow that could visit various locations around London and other major cities as well. The aim was to share good practice from the Jamaican experience, but also to listen to people on the ground to hear their concerns about these issues. I was eager to sound out public feeling and get firsthand insight into what was happening in Britain.

We entered a period of consultation and fact-finding, and began to plan what became known as the 'Guns on our streets' tour, which was organised in conjunction with Operation Trident, the Metropolitan Police's special unit that dealt with gun crimes within London's black community.[3] The mandate of Operation Trident fitted exactly with the things we were seeking to understand, so we were very keen for it to be involved. I spoke to one of the Trident superintendents and was put in contact with Detective Constable Ian Crichlow, who played a key role in the tour, presenting information from a police perspective. After the tour, DC Crichlow worked closely with me and others to found the initiative and clarify the core values of Street Pastors, so our relationship with Trident was very significant. Pastors Bobby Wilmot and Bruce Fletcher committed themselves to challenge the church in the UK to get involved in the problems of urban society. Bobby Wilmot described how churches in Kingston had begun to engage with people caught up in gun crime and how Christians had a responsibility to interact with them.[4]

The aims of the 'Guns on our streets' tour were these:

- to find out what help was already in place for affected communities.

- to establish a better grasp of the causes of gun crime.

---

3   For more on Operation Trident see chapter 7.
4   Reported in the Jamaican newspaper, *The Weekly Gleaner*, 19-25 June 2002.

- to see good practice in operation.

- to gather together the lessons that could be learned and begin to implement or contextualise them.

- to get the churches working together, but also to work with the police and local authorities to tackle this specific issue.

Another major landmark along the road at this time was a visit to Boston in the United States made by David Shosanya, one of our trustees.[5] At the time David was the pastor of Chalk Farm Baptist Church in North London, though he was soon to become Regional Minister for Mission in London for the Baptist Association. David was keen to see the work that was going on in Boston between the church and young gang members.

In Boston I saw firsthand what was dubbed as the 'Ten point coalition', formed by a group of local church ministers. They had been compelled to act in response to Scripture, specifically the words of Matthew 5:23–24—'Therefore, if you are offering your gift at the altar and there remember that your brother has something against you, leave your gift there in front of the

---

5   I am very grateful to David for his reflections on the development of the core values of Street Pastors in this and the following chapter. David has been instrumental in developing the initial vision of the Street Pastors initiative. Like me he has been on a journey, seeking to be practical in his Christian faith, and to bring to earth his intellectual and theological reflections. David grew up on an inner-city council estate in London, and he has a lot of insight into the challenges and needs of those communities. He has contributed a great deal to Street Pastors and to our ideas about how we bring the church and communities together.

altar. First go and be *reconciled* to your brother; then
come and offer your gift.'

David Shosanya

When we respond to these words, David argues, we give people
the chance to face up to their humanity and recognise it. Theologically,
this reinforces the concept of God's likeness in every human being,
something we often dismiss when we talk about people involved in
gangs, because it is all too easy to see them as less than human. Even
though these gang members were not an accepted part of the community, the pastors went to talk to them.

> These pastors understood that gang involvement is often
> the consequence of an individual's sense of exclusion
> from the community. Therefore, in the eyes of the gang
> members, the community has committed an offence
> against them. The church leaders took the scriptural
> imperative seriously, and resolved to make themselves
> available to talk and listen to these young people.
>
> *David Shosanya*

This gave the men the opportunity to become part of the community. David recounts how, when the Boston pastors connected
with these young men and women on the streets, 'they saw a big difference in the way the community responded. There was a grassroots
response because the church leaders had taken Scripture seriously.'

I wrote to the borough commanders (police chief superintendents)
of the areas that we were going to visit, inviting them to join us and

meet with other community leaders. Likewise I wrote to the chief executives of the local councils, also inviting them to come to the meeting and share their perspective. Invitations also went out to people in the community—parents, probation officers, social workers—so that we could hear from them firsthand. The tour was planned to include five boroughs in London: Southwark, Lambeth, Hackney/Tower Hamlets, Haringey and Brent. From London we went on to Birmingham and then to the areas of Moss Side and Longsight in Manchester. The pattern was a lunchtime reception or civic meeting, to which the police, youth leaders, social workers and council officers were invited, followed by an evening meeting open to the general public.

I gave a presentation about guns that was graphically illustrated by DC Ian Crichlow using police footage of crime scenes and victims of gun crime. These pictures powerfully brought home the realities of gun violence. DC Crichlow spoke of the fast-growing trend of drug- and gang-related crime.

> Gun crimes have tripled in London during the past year [2001–2] and there has been a rapid increase in teenagers purchasing guns, such that they appear to have become a fashion accessory … young men bond with the gun and gang as a means of finding material, social and emotional satisfaction. This culture has become their form of identity and self-worth … the gun brings them respect.

Pastor Bobby Wilmot and Pastor Bruce Fletcher also spoke about the Jamaican scenario. They described the absence of father figures for many young Jamaican men and referred to a notorious gang called 'The Fatherless Crew'. They also commented on the lack of education and high levels of illiteracy among gang members. They helped us to understand the urgency for action and gave the clear message that we must engage with the young men involved in gangs and gun crime on our own streets. 'Our success in Trench Town was achieved,' Wilmot said, 'because of the unity among the different bodies involved: the church leaders, and the communities with whom they worked as they sought to tackle the problem. One entity alone cannot achieve this.'[6]

Into the night

The response to these presentations and the tour as a whole was mixed, mainly a few degrees either side of lukewarm. Some of the London boroughs said, 'Thank you, but no thank you.' Some police officers were interested in hearing more about our proposals, but many believed it was their responsibility alone to deal with the problem. I subsequently learned that one police officer had commented, 'If this initiative is anything but a drain on the Met's resources, I will eat my hat.' He, and others like him, thought that we would be more of a liability than an asset, and thus create more problems for them. I recognised that the police and local authorities did not have my insights and that they had other priorities that must have been more pressing. As far as they were concerned, I had no track record and they were not used to seeing solutions come out of the church. The task of persuasion was a massive one.

---

6   Reported in *Christian Herald*, 6 July 2002.

Our message to the police was simple. We said, 'We have churches on nearly every high street. What service can they be to you and the community?' I firmly believe that the church exists not just for the benefits of its two-hour ministry on a Sunday morning (admittedly, if it's Pentecostal, it could be three hours), but to work for the good of society. So we were saying, 'Help us to understand what we need to do.' However, some officers' professional judgment was affected by their prejudices and scepticism towards Christians. Many didn't reply to my letter. Those officers who did come to the meeting found it quite insightful and refreshing because they hadn't realised the keenness and passion of Christians who were ready and willing to contribute to the safety of our community.[7]

The church response to the 'Guns on our streets' tour was also variable. In inviting church leaders to the tour, my plan had been to go to the top, to write or speak to the denominations at a national level, in the hope that the impact would filter down.

Some heads of denominations didn't respond to my invitation to contribute to the information-gathering purposes of the road-show, and I decided to follow up one of these, the invitation that had been made to George Carey, Archbishop of Canterbury. When I visited Church House, I discovered that my letter had been filed away under 'ethnic minorities'. The opinion of the community liaison officer that I spoke to that day was that this issue was a 'black' issue, not a societal issue. He told me, more or less, that he had so many things to deal with, he didn't have the capacity to respond to my concerns. I had hoped that the Anglican Church would do

---

7   The relationship we were able to develop with the Metropolitan Police is described fully in chapter 7.

some research into the issues and I asked whether it could be put on the agenda of the synod. That, apparently, could take two years! All hope of the Anglican Church picking up the issue faded away after this meeting.

Sadly, I also received no response from the Roman Catholic Church.[8] Over the next three years I did manage to meet with one or two of the denominational leaders. One of the most favourable responses we received was from the Baptist Association and its general secretary, David Coffey.[9]

The response from local government was very cold and sceptical. They couldn't get their head around the church wanting to do something. It wasn't our desire to have a practical role that was the problem, but the risk, as they saw it, that we would use the opportunity to preach. Many councils in London didn't reply to my letter, and initially these community bodies were very hard to reach. However, I kept informing them of my desire to work with them and to make the partnership effective. A few representatives came to our meetings. I didn't feel terribly discouraged. I knew I would have to prove myself to them. They were, of course, waiting to see if there was any mileage in these guys from Brixton. They would wait to see if we had sticking power.

---

8   However, one of the first people that came out with us on the streets at night was a Roman Catholic priest and an advisor to the then cardinal, Cormac Murphy-O'Connor. He lived in Pimlico. He said to me as we walked, 'Les, this is a completely different world to the one I live in. Yet it's just across the road from where I live.' I'll never forget how moved he was when he observed the tension on the streets. He was very excited that the church was taking this role, saying, 'I think people need to know about this initiative.'

9   I met David Coffey together with Wale Hudson-Roberts, the national racial justice coordinator for the Baptist Association of Great Britain, in Didcot at Baptist Association headquarters in 2003. They were very encouraging. They gave Ascension Trust £5,000 towards the work of Street Pastors. That was our first gift from a national body, and it enabled us to print our first brochure and get the initial group of street pastors trained. I am also deeply grateful to Roger and Faith Forster and the leaders of Ichthus Christian Fellowship in London, who continued to pay me as senior leader so that I could start this work, even though I had stepped down from leading a congregation.

Generally, the members of the public who came to one of the tour meetings were of one mind: they recognised that there was a problem, it was growing and something had to be done. As chair of the meetings, I was most surprised that these people—parents, grandparents, ordinary folk—were saying that the church had a role to play, and that if we would get involved, we could make a difference. Some expressed concerns about the safety issues connected with going out on the streets. One older gentleman, I remember, feared that he would not be accepted by young people on the street.[10]

At one meeting in Moss Side, Manchester, I heard people bemoaning the fact that the church was not playing its role in society. It was only looking after itself, they said, and it had made itself irrelevant. Among church leaders in Aston, Birmingham, the consensus was that these problems were isolated. Here, it was the police who were keen, and the churches who were denying the problems! Looking at this situation from a racial context, many black churches were not facing up to the realities of the problems on their doorstep, and white churches were unsure about the causes of the problem and what they could do to alleviate it.

It was at this time that I and others from Ascension Trust began to walk around communities at night to see what was going on. At a meeting with the borough commander for Lambeth, Chief Superintendent Dick Quinn, I asked about the challenges his officers faced at different times of the day. His reply was very informative. He

---

10 Repeatedly throughout the tour local people expressed concern about the marginalisation of black boys in the education system and the lack of good role models to counter the excess of negative role models. It was often noted that many resources were put into dealing with criminal behaviour instead of resourcing preventive initiatives. There was also much discussion about the church's current inactivity in contrast to its potential capacity to rally the black community (*Guns Off Our Streets* report, Ascension Trust, 2003).

identified two key sections of the day: the first was in the afternoon between 2 p.m. and 6 p.m. Between these hours, children and young people come out of school and college, and this gave rise to fear and anxiety in some communities where it was felt that young people were hanging around with nothing to occupy them. The commander told me that crime rates are very high at this time of day, but decline at 6 p.m. The second key time was between 10.30 p.m. and 3 a.m. Between these hours pubs close, alcohol takes effect, fights and muggings take place and vulnerable people are around. The nightlife tends to die down a bit around midnight as people go into clubs. Then around 2 a.m. trouble starts to increase again when the clubs empty out.

What did we learn from the tour and the meetings and conversations during that time? That many young people wanted to be engaged by adults, yet they felt polarised, experiencing a massive gap between them and the adult influences around them. I also began to recognise that there was a different world out there—an altogether different paradigm—on our streets at night time. That was most striking. In contrast to other Christian initiatives that required people to come to a venue, on someone else's terms, I began to see that the work I wanted to do would be done outside a building and, specifically, within these night time hours.

CHAPTER FIVE

WITHOUT PREACHING OR PREJUDICE

Lambeth Life, December 2004

Core values

The 'Guns on our streets' tour was a way of establishing whether we were on the right path. When it finished we were left with a large quantity of information and feedback that needed to be pulled together. And so, towards the end of 2002, I met with David Shosanya and DC Ian Crichlow of Operation Trident, both of whom had been significantly involved in the tour, to work through the findings. We began by deciding that what we had learned was not going to be consigned to the archives; we would act upon it. Unanimously we agreed that this response needed concrete solutions and strategies. Our concern to act in a practical way was a priority.

We discussed the question, 'What are we asking the church to do?' The answer that came back was that we were asking the church to go onto the streets at night, to engage with people and to listen to them. What was the message that we wanted Christians to articulate on the street? We were very concerned that street preaching or explicit evangelism did not find its way onto the agenda. Therefore it was critical that people understood what we wanted to do. David Shosanya formed a list of core values to underpin the proposals for action:

- The sacredness and the sanctity of human life.

- The importance of valuing and honouring our community. We should take pride in the place where we live.

- The development of integrity. Integrity is a vital part of the fabric of society.

- The desire to take personal responsibility. Some people blame others all too easily. They blame their parents, their environment or other people for the reason that they do the things they do. We need to help people to understand that they do not have to become victims of their own circumstances.

- The development of individuals to their fullest potential. We believe that each individual can make a major contribution to society. Others can help that awareness to grow.

Our core values would be like tram lines to keep our focus and help us travel in the right direction. David Shosanya has referred to these statements as 'a natural and valid entry point' for the church to speak into the debate around crime, violence and its effects on society as a whole.[1] 'Importantly,' David explains, 'they are as culturally relevant as they are theologically relevant. They are also relevant to African and Caribbean history. Honouring and valuing community is rooted in the African concept of *ubuntu*—"I am only a person through other persons"—and this sense of an individual being rooted in other people has its own dynamic equivalent in the Caribbean community. Yet, as a whole package they are universal values that could be true of any culture. They hold a high premium in African and Caribbean communities but, because they are also rooted in Scripture, they do not exclude other communities.'

> Irrespective of people's dislocation and disenfranchisement, I believe that there is always a core of connection to community, if not through a parent, perhaps through a grandmother, aunt or uncle. Many individuals may appear feral but they still have a residue of connection. In our postmodernist society where the historic sense of belonging to Christianity is receding, we will not get those people into church. We have to meet them in their own space. There is a biblical imperative to go to where they are (see Matt. 22:1–14).
>
> As we formed the core values of the Street Pastors initiative we were essentially formalising years of ministry that we had been involved in and turning it into a structured

1   *Guns Off Our Streets* report, Appendix D.

concept. In one sense it was really a Christian version
of street work, or detached youth ministry, but it was
packaged in a way Christians could understand. We had
confidence in the idea.

Ascension Trust collected these contributions into a report called
Guns Off Our Streets, which was presented to the board of trustees.
The report came out of a significant process of evaluation, during
which the Trust took the time to develop a response that would not
be a knee-jerk reaction but would be comprehensive. We wanted
to make a robust response to the data that had been produced and
the anecdotal comments made by the ministers from Jamaica. It was
also important that our response had the backing of church leaders,
and that we affirmed the convictions we had heard from the general
public about the way that the church should respond. We needed to
be innovative but consultative.

The report went on to outline the Jamaican experience and
perspective. It detailed the economic and physical condition of the
capital city, Kingston, and described the area as a place in need of
significant government investment.[2] Figures for murders, attempted
murders and shooting incidents in London, sourced from Operation
Trident, were also included.[3]

January–August 2002 (in comparison with the same
period in 2001):

---

2   *Guns Off Our Streets* report, 4.
3   *Guns Off Our Streets* report, Appendix C. Figures are also given for the age of Trident victims in the period January to August
    2002, and the venue of Trident incidents (vehicle, street, nightclub, etc).

Murder   14% increase

Attempted murder 8% increase

Other shooting incidents   98% increase (43 incidents
                                              up to 85 incidents)

Total incidents   47% increase

Although the core values were formed in 2002 in response to the issues of guns and gangs, they express the ethos of the initiative that every Street Pastors team commits to when they go out onto the streets, whatever the needs of their community are. All over the country, however the antisocial behaviour manifests itself, our core values are integral to the individual street pastor's role.

At the same time as we established our core values, we also turned our attention towards the name we should give to the volunteers who were to go out on the streets. There were two main things to note: first, streets full of problems and, second, people needing someone to care for them and demonstrate hope to them. The word *pastor* was suggested, not in the sense of ordination, but in its literal meaning, 'shepherd', 'carer'. From there it was a small step to the name 'street pastor'. We knew we had struck upon the right thing!

Whose problem is it?

In the wake of the 'Guns on our streets' tour, we knew we had to get the churches on board. Whatever the response was from them, it was important that we made a sustained effort to keep local

churches informed and encourage their participation with Street
Pastors. I sent out a letter to church leaders informing them about
the 'Guns on our streets' tour and the information we had gathered, with the clear message that this issue should not be hidden
away in a box labelled 'urban' or 'black': it applied to all of us, and
needed all of us to apply ourselves to it in response. Gun and knife
crime has the potential to impact the whole of society, I wrote,
and we need all traditions of church to get on board because of the
sheer enormity of the problem.

I encouraged churches to think about their theological response
to the issues that drugs, guns and gangs were raising. For me it was
important that this theological understanding was in place because
it would affect how churches saw their role in terms of their commitment to the community and their strategy for response. In asking
questions of church leaders about their response to social problems,
I wanted churches to examine how they used their buildings and
resources—could they be used as part of the solutions to the needs of
our communities? What will you do, I asked, that will engage people
in a basic, practical way?

A small number of church leaders replied to me and some
of them admitted that they hadn't got a theological or practical
response to the needs of their communities. In general, however,
the response to the letter was very disappointing. The silence said
several things to me. First, church leaders are busy people; not
everything makes it to the top of their inbox. Second, it said that
Christians do not understand the problem, or they believe it is
someone else's problem (one that could be left to the police or even
to ethnic minority communities). Third, it said to me they may be

fearful of the unknown and uncertain about the connections with other power structures that we were encouraging them towards.

We also invited churches to a reception at Brixton Baptist Church, where the *Guns Off Our Streets* report was outlined and made available. Churches were invited to partner in the initiative. There was a strong response from those that attended, with a genuine recognition that something practical was needed. However, several church leaders we had expected to be present were not, so overall we felt that the response from churches was quite weak. This cautiousness had the knock-on effect of making the initiative less accessible for those people in the pew. What we needed at that point were advocates who were in senior positions in the church. In general, there was a sigh of relief that someone had come up with an idea, but there was also a lack of commitment in terms of resources.

The Aston shootings

On New Year's Day 2003 my wife, Louise, and I paid our customary visit to my in-laws. At the end of the day we would always pray together, as an extended family, to reflect on the past year and give thanks. I remember feeling a heaviness in my heart for the young people of this generation. I outlined my concerns, as we each in turn presented our hopes and fears to the Lord in prayer. I prayed and confessed, 'Lord, the church has not fully grasped the magnitude of the problem.'

The following day, concerns about guns and gangs were not just voiced in my in-laws' front room, but in front rooms up and down the country. On 2 January, every news channel and every newspaper carried headlines about the shooting of four young girls, two fatally, in Aston, Birmingham. My phone was ringing like crazy: journalists and church leaders alike were asking, 'Les, we know you have been talking about this; what do we do?' One of the first calls I received that morning was from Pastor Calvin Young from Aston Christian Centre in Birmingham. He apologised to me for the lack of interest among churches in his community who, the year before, had not wanted to be part of the 'Guns on our streets' roadshow. 'The media have descended on us,' he said. 'They are asking for interviews. How should we handle it?' His associate minister, Pastor Sandra Thomas, then came on the phone to me. She was about to be interviewed on breakfast TV. At the same time a lot of young people were turning up at Aston Christian Centre in shock and despair, needing counselling.

A minor dispute at an all-night party escalated into the gun battle between two drugs gangs which left two girls wounded, it emerged yesterday.

The dead girls stood little chance as the self-styled 'Burger Bar Boys' and the 'Johnson Crew' exchanged more than 30 shots from at least three weapons, one a sub-machine gun.

The 'Burger Bar Boys' had reigned in parts of Birmingham for over a decade, but the battle for the growing drugs trade had generated increasing violence.

Daily Telegraph, 4 January 2003

It was as if everything we had been talking about had suddenly manifested itself. It was suddenly right in everyone's face and questions were being asked. It felt as if every journalist had just one assignment that week. The fatal shooting of teenagers Charlene Ellis and Letisha Shakespeare was a turning point in terms of the media and the wider society asking questions about drugs, guns and gangs.

That same day I spoke to senior church leaders, to Joel Edwards, the then general secretary of the Evangelical Alliance (EA), and to Mark Sturge, who was then chief executive of the African and Caribbean Evangelical Alliance (ACEA). Immediately, Mark and I issued a press release as a response from the black churches. At the weekend, Joel Edwards, a journalist named Marcia Dixon and I travelled to Birmingham to attend the Sunday morning service at Aston Christian Centre. There must have been well over a hundred young people who attended in addition to the normal congregation, simply because of the emotional turmoil they were experiencing. The atmosphere in the church was one of shock. Young people were asking, could this happen to me?

What we realised that weekend was the magnitude of the devastation that had hit the community, especially the young people. In fact, I think there was a significant change of perception in that community from that time. First, people began to take the problem seriously. Second, they recognised that there was a lot of work to be done. Third, there was an acknowledgement that the problems were complex and deep-seated. Many people realised that these problems had been developing for a long time under their noses and would take years to solve. That terrible loss of life galvanised people. Pastor Calvin Young expressed it like this:

I want a massive change in our community in how we relate to each other and work with each other. We need to change the system so that young people don't feel they have to find gangs to find identity. As a community we must give them an identity, tell them their worth, and make sure they are educated so that their potential can be developed. And I want churches to work together so that we can bring God back into the lives of our people.[4]

There was talk of a major event to bring the community together at Aston Villa football stadium in only two weeks' time. It was incredibly short notice to organise an event of that size, but the local people were of one mind and anything was possible. Two weeks later, several thousands of people made their way to the stadium and witnessed an excellent programme of musicians and speakers. The bishop of Birmingham was there, together with leaders from the Muslim and Hindu communities. It was in this national context that Street Pastors was born.

Unanswered questions

At the launch of Street Pastors just three weeks later, on 28 January 2003, Calvin Young and Sandra Thomas spoke about the impact of gun crime on their community. Paul Keeble, who had been involved in the 'Gangstop' march in Manchester, brought reports from his community, sometimes referred to in the press as 'Gunchester'. Inspector Bob Pull from the Metropolitan Police talked about the

---

4   Interviewed in *The Voice*, 3 March 2003.

police perspective. Roger Forster, the leader of Ichthus Christian Fellowship, shared a reflection on the need for a Christian response. I laid out the proposal and the concept behind Street Pastors. The shootings at Aston had been a catalyst, bringing the issue of our blighted cities to the forefront.

The launch was a sober event. We sought to be informative, to communicate the fact that if we didn't do anything, things would get worse. The emphasis was on the fact that we must do some-thing because we have the grace, power, conviction and love of our Lord Jesus Christ. Some thought we were too ambitious. In a time like this, I thought, we need ambitious people, people with strong conviction. Still it was difficult for many church leaders to see their role in Street Pastors. I truly hoped that I had said nothing that might make people think we were asking them to take part in another 'mission'!

I came away from the launch feeling optimistic because the event had attracted a good number of church leaders from a variety of denominations. However, it soon became clear that there were still unanswered questions for many, and the number who turned up for our first training session was very small. On top of this, there was scepticism in some sectors of the general public, as evidenced by opinions gathered for the London newspaper *The Voice* the day before the launch.[5]

> I don't think many people are going to like it. People generally go out to enjoy themselves and forget about

---

5   As recorded in *The Voice*, 27 January 2003.

their troubles. To have preachers in their faces about it at a club may irk nerves a bit. It's a noble idea, but I don't think it's going to work. I think the black churches can help, but people need to want to be helped first. What people really need is a wake-up call.

Layla Powell, 21, model, Waterloo

I would be shocked to see a preacher in a club. However, I think it would grab people's attention about how serious this violence is getting. Most people would start laughing or cussing if some preacher came up to them talking about gun violence. I don't think Christians should think it's their responsibility to stop gang violence. Not everyone is going to embrace Christianity as they would embrace an effort to end gun violence.

Anastasia Bonsu, 16, student, Kilburn

When I'm at a club, hanging out with my friends, the last thing I want is someone coming up to me and preaching. No one will listen to some preacher at a rave. The pastors should go somewhere else where people would be more likely to listen, like schools and youth clubs where younger children can look up to more positive role models and follow them.

Jerome Henry, 22, student, Dulwich

I decided to do some canvassing of my own. Accompanied by a reporter from the BBC, who had been given an assignment to gauge people's response to Street Pastors, I walked around Brixton one evening around 10 p.m. I received some negative responses and a lot of questions, for example, 'Would a street pastor be a police informer?' Generally people thought the idea was pretty good, as long as street pastors were going to be relevant, and not preach at people telling them how bad they were. Many people said that the only thing they had ever heard a preacher saying was that they were a sinner.

In a pub just off Atlantic Road in Brixton, I introduced myself to the manager and explained who I was. Then contrary to our agreement that she would stay as low-key as possible, the BBC reporter produced an enormous microphone and asked the manager what she thought about Street Pastors. Inevitably a crowd began to form. People didn't like the idea that Brixton was always in the news as a troublespot, and one guy in particular came across to me, with defiance in his eyes. I asked him whether he had heard of Street Pastors. 'Yes, I've heard of you people,' he replied. 'You are the ones that are going to be the eyes and ears of the police.' I calmly said, 'No, this is a church initiative.' He kept on aggressively saying that we were going to be informers and generally created a bit of commotion in the pub. The journalist loved it! I had to hold my ground and use all my skills to convey our intentions, not only to this man, but also to everybody else who was listening. Then people began to warm to what I was saying. I prayed for Brixton and everybody in that bar and that greatly diffused the tension. However, it was clear that we had to overcome the perception among many that we were not going to be informers of the police.

The urban trinity

The street pastor's role is to care, listen and help. Caring means we are physically there with people on the streets. Listening means it is not about me—what I have come to say—but about another person being heard. Helping is a tangible, practical thing. That raised a very important and critical question in our discussion that night: many Christians wouldn't know what to do if someone said to them, 'I want to give you a gun or knife.' Many wouldn't know what to do if someone said, 'I'm in a gang and I want to get out.' This was one reason that we felt the church needed to be in partnership with other community agencies. As I thought through that concept of partnership, I realised that the three biggest structures in any city, when it comes to power and resources, are the local government, the police and the church. I was convinced that these three had to do more than just drink tea together at a mayoral reception.

The issues our society faces are massive, and this also tells me that no one single group or organisation can tackle them successfully. We need to work in partnership, because failure to do so means that the criminals are the only ones doing any joined-up thinking! Where gangs and gang culture are concerned, government-sponsored research has found that these groups know how to motivate their members, and their operations are highly organised and structured.

> Britain's inner-city street gangs are run like successful businesses: efficient, well-organised and respectful of authority, according to a Nottingham study.

[Researchers] found some gangs are so highly motivated that they could match the drive of any big corporation. 'Good' workers were promoted to more lucrative and responsible positions within the gang.

The Voice, 28 July 2003

I first became aware of the phrase 'urban trinity' as I read a book called *The Urban Christian*, written by Ray Bakke.[6] It was during the civil unrest of the 1960s that Bakke and his young family moved into a poverty-stricken neighbourhood of Chicago, and he lived out his faith in the inner city in a way that was both matter-of-fact and inspirational. He wrote about transforming people not only spiritually but economically and educationally too. Bakke did some analysis of the city of Chicago and looked at the different people groups and what they brought to the community. Of particular interest to me were his comments about the Irish immigrant group. He believed they were a people who had knowledge of and influence in three sectors of society. He said the Irish understood politics (because of their dealings with British government), they understood policing (because they saw the power of the police) and they understood the role of the priest. When I recalled Bakke's thesis about the way in which the Irish entered into all three roles, I was convinced that to really be effective, we needed this kind of tripartite base.

For me, partnership means that the church, the police and local government aim to complement and support each other for the benefit of the community. This means that we will each need

---

6   Ray Bakke, *The Urban Christian*. 'Effective Ministry in Today's Urban World' (InterVarsity Press/Marc Europe, 1987).

to acknowledge our differences of role and function within communities. I believed this kind of thinking had been lacking for many years in Britain. Chapter 7 will look at the early relationship between Street Pastors and the police, and chapter 8 describes how we struggled to establish the interdenominational church response that is at the core of Street Pastors today. Before that, in chapter 6, I will go on to outline how we were received by local authorities in our priority boroughs in London.

CHAPTER SIX

MORE LIKELY TO BE TRUSTED

What Works' in Community Cohesion, Department for Communities and Local
Government, June 2007

The local government response

A successful relationship with council leaders and executives will
not happen overnight. Even as the credibility of Street Pastors has
increased, with Street Pastors referenced in local government committee reports and publications (evidenced in the chapter title above),
responses from councils are very patchy and variable. Today, as at
the beginning of the initiative, local authorities often watch from a
distance, observing our relationship with the police and what happens on the streets. Clearly, then as now, we have to prove ourselves.

The relationship between the church and local government has
historically been a tense one. They have been suspicious of each
other. When you look at the recent history of British politics, there
are periods when a liberal agenda has clashed with Christian values,
with the effect of polarising church and government. When I went

along to meetings with local authorities, instead of hearing what I was saying about today's challenges, councillors and officials were recalling past tensions. Local authorities looked at me and saw a man going out into public places to talk about religion. They saw a black man, a minister of the church, and straight away they assumed I would be preaching and telling everyone they are sinners. Could they trust me? Could they be seen to be working with me? Many of the councils that we wanted to work with were very suspicious and cold. In some cases we were told explicitly that they did not want to fund an exclusively Christian organisation, and this is still the case with some councils.

I had assumed we would receive a warmer welcome, and I was taken aback. Equally disappointing were the times that I would have a good meeting with someone, ending with a promise of future contact, but then the link would go cold, with nothing more to be heard from them.

In the months after the launch of Street Pastors we began exploring the ways in which we could work with the boroughs we had covered during the 'Guns on our streets' tour. After Lambeth and Hackney, Lewisham was the third borough in London where Street Pastors began to operate. Looking back to March 2004 when Eustace Constance, the coordinator for Lewisham, began to establish a relationship with the borough council, we can see the extent of the effort that was needed. The first few months of Eustace's work in Lewisham produced a diary full of meetings with local council representatives. He met with many civic and administrative key players in the borough, such as the Lord Mayor, Lewisham Community Sector officers, local housing officers and the Anti-Social Behaviour Action Team. Ascension Trust was represented at town hall forums at which crime, graffiti and police dispersal powers were discussed, and Eustace also attended public meetings held with local councillors.

In general terms, we have learnt that a good relationship with the local authority is probably one that starts with the council expressing reservations and concerns, but having a readiness to test out a pilot scheme followed by evaluation and monitoring.[1] During this period, we have the opportunity to say to the council, 'How can we help you to be effective?' In the strongest relationships there might also be discussion about the council's role in providing funding for the training of street pastors. Long-term support and evaluation, with regular meetings to see how we are getting on, is also appropriate and helpful.

> We met Joe again—had not seen him since Christmas. Joe is an addict who begs outside the Venue. His dog died on New Year's Eve, he has just been kicked out of his squat and is homeless again, although he manages to stay for a night or two in a friend's home. We called Street Rescue, who reminded us that he had to stay out for a week in the same spot to be considered a 'rough sleeper'. I told him the rules and suggested that he goes to Crisis Recovery the next morning for a hot drink and to let them know where he would be staying. This way we could contact Street Rescue again and get

---

1   See chapter 3 for examples of local authority evaluation of Street Pastors.

him into a hostel hopefully by next week. The follow-up
was successful—Street Rescue was able to pick him
up.

Street pastor, Deptford

It is also useful for local authorities to gather their own feed-back from the streets and from local businesses, particularly those involved in the night time economy, for example, pub licencees and club doormen. Another measure of our success is the public response, and many people do take the time to talk to the council. Rates of referral to local authority agencies are another guide.[2] Frequently, street pastors meet homeless people and get involved in referring them to hostels, using a list of sheltered accommodation for the relevant borough and neighbouring ones. A street pastor is able to make a phone call and then to find out where there are beds for the night or which shelter could take this person on long-term. We have discovered many different agencies provide beds, but sometimes there is no central network to show where empty beds are. Although at first the lack of beds seems to be the main obstacle to getting people off the streets, it is in many cases the tracking down of a bed that is more problematic. There are more places than first appear, but the data is not linked up. When the council gives us an accommodation list we are able to interpret the information so that it is more user-friendly.

---

2   Research carried out as part of the evaluation of Portsmouth Street Pastors indicates the following breakdown for referrals: 48 percent of people requested a Street Pastors card; 32 percent required a faith-related referral; 13 percent of people wanted help in connection to homelessness; 3 percent of contacts accepted a referral in connection with alcohol and drugs; 2 percent of contacts accepted a referral in connection with mental health. (Figures were obtained from street pastors' diaries, from 155 contacts made during the period July 2007 to July 2008.)

Came across Robert at approximately 2.30 a.m. He was trying to sleep in the doorway of the Salvation Army building on Deptford High Street. He had been kicked out of his girlfriend's flat a week ago and had slept on the street ever since. He was her carer, so he lost his lodging, job and all his belongings, including his ID papers, all in one go. He does not drink or take drugs. He was very cold so we went to The Bear Church and made him a cup of tea. Found him a sleeping bag. We prayed for him and the next morning a local church took him in, fed him, kept him that night and the next morning.

Street Pastors helped him sort out accommodation. He was assessed by the Salvation Army that same day and was accepted on the spot. We are in touch with him on a regular basis. He is doing well, seeking training to find a new career. Street Rescue could not provide him with a bed until he had ID papers, so they helped him get some new documents together. He was referred to the Crisis Recovery workshop at Deptford Churches, where he is continuing to receive support.

Street pastor, Deptford

Street pastors also have a role to play as intermediary between people on the street and local government. We often find rough sleepers who have tried to find themselves a bed for the night, or a more permanent shelter, but they find there are too many bureaucratic

hoops for them to jump through. Some people feel that nobody wants
to see them at the council, or that nobody is listening to them or has
the time to guide them through the process. A street pastor can make
arrangements to meet up with that person in daytime hours, take them
to the housing office and give them the help and representation that
they need. The better the relationship between Street Pastors and the
local council, the more effective the signposting will be.

> Bureaucracy keeps some people away from Homeless
> Persons Units and housing offices. Plus, each agency
> has a different list of criteria, and the people who need
> to access their help can't deal with the paperwork. In
> the borough of Lewisham, we have tried to identify
> places that will take direct referrals without too much
> bureaucracy.

> On one occasion I was contacted by a police officer who
> needed someone to meet a man due to leave Belmarsh
> Prison that day. The officer told me that if the man wasn't
> met by someone, he would very likely go straight to the
> pub, get drunk, get into a fight, be unable to collect his
> clothes and paperwork from the different offices where
> they were held, and pretty soon he would be back to
> square one. Arrangements were made for the man
> to be kept in a holding cell until I got there. However,
> something went wrong and the man was released alone.
> Amazingly, he approached my car as I looked for the
> right entrance to the prison, tapped on the window and

asked if I was Eustace! Together we were able to collect
his clothes and money, and then I helped him through
the form-filling at the Homeless Persons Unit. He was
processed that day and settled that day.

Eustace Constance

A significant milestone for us was the publication in December
2004 of a double-page article in the local government newspaper,
Lambeth Life. The very positive report about Street Pastors in South
London included a logo depicting the 'urban trinity' (borough of
Lambeth-Metropolitan Police-church) with this caption:

The Local Authority provides education and social services. The Police maintain law and order. The church has
a spiritual, caring role. Each one has responsibility for
the welfare of the community.

The church was described as 'providing a new spiritual and moral
solution to urban problems':

[Street pastors] provide a calming influence where tension exists, instilling values and social conscience back
into communities. They act as a buffer, a bridge and
intermediary or referral service for people who need it
… They are gaining respect in the communities in which
they serve, partly down to the fact that they have no
agenda, no ulterior motive, other than to care.

Lambeth Life

Some local authorities are still not interested, but we have generally moved from a cold dismissal of what Street Pastors could offer to a position where our integrity and passion are acknowledged.

In September 2004 one Street Pastors team was joined by Michael Howard MP, the leader of the Conservative Party at the time. His late-night tour of Brixton, accompanied by myself and other street pastors, received wide coverage in the press. Some viewed it as an attempt to 'court the black vote', others as no more than a photo opportunity to improve the leader's image.[3] However, Mr Howard's endorsement of our work and his broader comments about releasing 'the energy that exists in local communities' in order to be an influence for good were very welcome.[4]

---

3   Reports appeared in *The Voice*, 27 September 2004, and the *Evening Standard*, 20 September 2004. A photograph of Mr Howard with street pastors was also used in an article attacking Mr Howard's record on immigration and asylum in the *Evening Standard*, 19 April 2005.
4   *The Voice*, 27 September 2004.

CHAPTER SEVEN

GOD'S COPS
Lancashire Evening Post, 2 September 2008

Police partnership

After the launch in January 2003, we began to further develop our relationship with the police. We were greatly helped by Chief Inspector Leroy Logan (also chairman of the Black Police Officers Association) and Inspector Bob Pull, who very much believed in what we were doing. As police officers, and Christian police officers, they caught the vision in a much bigger way than church leaders did. They were very eager to help in whatever way they could. Inspector Pull was instrumental in preparing us to begin discussions with the police. I remember chatting to him in my office, and asking him, 'What should we be asking the police for?' At a meeting on 29 March, CI Logan and Inspector Pull informed Eustace Constance and me about the expectations of the Metropolitan Police regarding risk assessments and procedures for the handing-in of weapons to street pastors. It was suggested that I should keep both officers informed about the boroughs we would be working in, so that they could liaise with borough commanders on our behalf. Both men expressed the belief that it was God's will for them to be involved in the initiative. I give God thanks for the role that they played in establishing our relationship with the police. CI Logan was very proactive about the training aspects of our relationship with the Met, and both he and Inspector Pull contributed significantly to the training of our street pastors in the first four years.

I joined the Metropolitan Police in London in 1976 and twenty years later, after promotion to police inspector, I had a life-changing experience and became a Christian. Initially I didn't think my newfound faith would have an impact on crime; after all, it was a personal thing, and within the police service at the time it wasn't something you were encouraged to talk about. But after becoming a Christian a number of things happened.

The first was an unquenchable desire to bring communities together and build bridges between communities and the police. Second was my appointment to the office of chairman of the Christian Police Association (Metropolitan Branch), and the third was the opportunity to work in partnership with the Street Pastors initiative.

I remember reading a newspaper article about pastors who were used as peacemakers in various American cities. It made me think of 'Peacemakers who sow in peace raise a harvest of righteousness' (James 3:18). This kindled a response in my heart: why couldn't this happen here in the UK? I was totally unaware at this stage that an ex-Rastafarian called Les Isaac was having similar thoughts.

One morning, in my office on the ninth floor of New Scotland Yard, I noticed a flier for the launch of the Street Pastors initiative at Brixton Baptist Church. It was here that I first met Les and a fellow cop, Detective Constable Ian Crichlow, who was working with Operation Trident, a police-led response to murder and gun crime in the capital. My spirit just leapt as I heard about this opportunity for Christians to make an impact on policing, and as I realised that senior detectives saw the value of engaging with Christians as part of the solution.

I knew that I could help in respect of providing assistance, advice and training. There were many questions: what were the risks? What training was necessary? What about the safety of volunteers? Insurance? What protocols between the police and Street Pastors were necessary?

Bob Pull, former police inspector
Diversity Directorate New Scotland Yard,
Metropolitan Police, 1999–2005

Trident is an anti-gun operation set up by the Met in 1998 to help bring an end to shootings and murders among young black Londoners, working through partnership with community leaders and robust, intelligence-based policing.[1] Around the time of the launch of Street Pastors and our initial talks with the police, the Met was claiming an improvement in the number of gun-related incidents in London and stronger relationships with the capital's black communities, although Home Office figures released in January 2003 still showed that gun crime had risen by 35 percent in the twelve months prior to April 2002.[2] Nonetheless, there was a commitment on the part of the police to continue to work with community groups and make clear that giving young men 'other avenues' for self-esteem to replace the possession of a gun was the responsibility of the whole community, not just the police.[3] DC Crichlow from the Operation Trident unit was a key figure of the 'Guns on our streets' tour and was also part of the discussions that followed, out of which came the core values of Street Pastors.

I could see that in the early days—perhaps the first two years of the life of the initiative—the police were waiting to see if we could prove ourselves. Although they were warmer to us than borough councils, we clearly had to convince the upper tiers of the hierarchy. Lambeth borough commander, Chief Superintendent Dick Quinn, was a larger-than-life guy, very creative and willing to try whatever tools he had at his disposal. I guess he knew that he had major

---

1   See www.stoptheguns.org and www.met.police.uk/scd/specialist_units/trident.htm. In 2003, officers from Operation Trident investigated more than 100 shootings, including eleven murders. For the role of Operation Trident in the presentation of the 'Guns on our streets' tour, see chapter 4.

2   www.bbc.co.uk/1/hi/uk/2834993.stm, 12 January 2003.

3   www.bbc.co.uk/1/hi/uk/2834993.stm, 2 December 2004.

challenges in Lambeth, and Street Pastors might just be able to help him deal with them. When I approached him with my concerns about protocol and safety, and my desire to clarify our position in respect of firearms, he responded by instructing one of his officers, Inspector Sean Wilson (now chief inspector), to produce a working document and present it to Scotland Yard and the Home Office for them to consider its implications.[4]

The draft document set out the 'difficulties and options for using intermediaries to facilitate the surrender of illegally held firearms'.[5] The surrender of weapons was a critical element in our relationship with the Metropolitan Police; we were already operating in two London boroughs and based on this experience—and the belief that Street Pastors would provide a challenge to some people to walk away from their wrongdoing—an agreement with the police was vital. I believed that street pastors would encounter people just like Zacchaeus, who declared that if he had taken anything from anyone, he wanted to give it back (Luke 19:8). We felt that the chances of someone other than the person in possession of the weapon—a mother, perhaps, or a girlfriend—coming across a gun or knife were high, and that for this reason there were a variety of routes through which street pastors might be involved in the surrender of a weapon. I had already heard of a case where a man had brought a machine gun to church to give to the pastor, and another, where a gun had been left at the altar. Elsewhere, drugs had been brought to church and

---

4   I am very grateful to Chief Inspector Wilson who, together with Michelle Elkins from the East Area Press Office, generously assisted me in the analysis of the early events in the relationship between Street Pastors and the Metropolitan Police.

5   *The Discussion Paper on Third Party Surrender of Firearms* was drafted by Detective Sergeant John Webb, and dated 11 February 2004.

surrendered. Wherever God is moving, things beyond our human understanding always happen.

As time went by I realised that, for the Met, this process required an extraordinary blend of innovation and detailed scrutiny. The draft document shows that their considerations of the surrender of weapons to a third party ranged widely, from the maintenance of the independence and integrity of Street Pastors to general legal principles and risk management. The paper then outlined four options for London and the pros and cons of each.

CI Sean Wilson, who at the time had responsibility for Brixton town centre, recalls the policing context in the borough in 2003:

> There were two big issues: street crime and drug dealing. Drug dealers were very prominent at this time. This was partially due to cartels, essentially Jamaican, which were expanding rapidly, as Jamaicans didn't need a visa to travel to the UK. The Met's partnership work was very institutionalised at this time. If it didn't have an institution attached to it (for example, a local government agency) then although we would work with the voluntary sector, it attracted less of our attention. Funding was a big issue here. In this respect, we didn't think outside the box enough. Yet there was a lot of political interest in policing at this time. A number of prominent politicians visited Brixton to see the issues at firsthand for themselves.

It was following the circulation of this discussion paper that CI Wilson arranged a meeting for us at Scotland Yard. Sergeant Tony

Unthank, from the Community Safety Team in Lewisham, met Eustace and me outside Scotland Yard on the day of the meeting. There were a number of officers around the table, together with Home Office civil servant Carole Eniffer. I gave them some background on Street Pastors—what we were and what we weren't—tried not to be too 'churchy' and talked for about twenty-five minutes. It was clear that everyone there that day had given thought to the whole thing. We had a collective starting point: we all wanted weapons off the streets, and our priority was the safety of our volunteers. However, let's be realistic, we were approaching this issue from very different places. Some of the initial reactions to the concept of Street Pastors from the Metropolitan Police are summed up in the words of CI Wilson:

> When I took the phone call from Les, my first reaction was that people who could be effective on the streets were people who were accustomed to the drugs environment: that plainly wasn't Street Pastors. I thought their chances of success were limited. I had big reservations about safety. If it wasn't managed safely Street Pastors would be another statistic. In effect, street pastors would be intruding on a drug dealer's 'patch', and they would be out of their depth and extremely vulnerable.
>
> I was also concerned that the arrival of street pastors might mean that drug-related activities were simply displaced and would take over another area. I knew that the people street pastors would encounter would only be

the pawns; they would not have any influence over the guys earning the big money who did not live in the area.

Initially I was sceptical. I thought it would involve a lot of work on our part for very little positive result.

When we went back for our second meeting, the officers who had drawn up the draft paper had made contact with forces around the world to investigate their experiences of the surrender of weapons through intermediaries.[6] The most interesting response came from South Africa, where community-based organisations had occasionally been used to facilitate the handing-in of guns. A group of elders had encouraged a lot of gunmen to give up their guns and throw them in the river. During the night, however, other men had dived in and fished them all out!

We made every effort to use the right language—the language of citizenship—making clear our identity (we are not an add-on to the police), and articulating our belief that there was a gap in community and police relations that Street Pastors could fill. We didn't want to be the police. We made it clear that we were the church, not a bunch of James Bond wannabes or *Charlie's Angels* throwbacks. Where police officers were too busy to stop and listen to someone, we could draw alongside; where police officers had to be disciplinarians, we could be carers. We wanted to serve our community, and we wanted to do it with policies and procedures.

---

6 Police departments in Canada, Australia, New Zealand, South Africa and France were consulted. Details were given of the schemes that operated in the US, including 'buy-back' schemes, where a weapon could be surrendered anonymously to a police station in exchange for cash, and long-standing amnesty programmes.

All my concerns were geared around safety and liability, because we had a duty of care to Street Pastors. Yet, there was another side of me that thought, this is so very different and out of the ordinary, it might just work! What intrigued me was that street pastors had a uniform, which they bought themselves. Also, when I attended the commissioning service in Westminster, I couldn't comprehend the number of Christians who were gathered there. I had no experience of this element of the community before that time.

Chief Inspector Sean Wilson

The emphasis at this second meeting was on the need for clear procedures when a weapon of any kind was handed to a street pastor. There were risks for the police and for us. We agreed that not every street pastor would be authorised to surrender weapons, only one appropriate person from every team. If a street pastor came into possession of a firearm, no action would be taken against them by the police as long as certain conditions were met.

In some instances, without clarification, it could have been illegal for street pastors to possess some or all of these items. It took a long time for Les to get the police and Crown Prosecution Service to agree to the protocols. I knew this would be the case, purely because of the size of the organisations he was engaging with.

Bob Pull, former police inspector

The Draft Agreement

The Draft Agreement between the Metropolitan Police Service and Ascension Trust was produced in April 2004.[7] The officers involved worked hard to write and rewrite it, pass it over to us and work on it again when we passed it back. There was a massive amount of consultation to be done. The agreement outlined the circumstances in which it would apply, the underlying principles and the details of the working relationship between the Met and Ascension Trust.[8]

> Ascension Trust will nominate a senior street pastor as a point of contact for police in every borough where they intend to operate. The senior street pastor will notify police of the number of street pastors being deployed, of the area they will be in and the times between which they will be working on every occasion they go out. They will also inform police when they withdraw from the area. The street pastors will wear their distinctive jackets and caps while they are working. The street pastors undertake to call police immediately if they come across any incident in which the life or safety of any individual is in danger, or where private property is at risk of serious damage. The street pastors acknowledge their civic duty to assist in the prevention and detection of crime.

---

7   For the first year in the life of Street Pastors we operated without any agreement with the police.

8   The 'Underlying Principles' state, 'The MPS and Ascension Trust agree that it is the civic duty of every person to do what they can to prevent crime.'

> The street pastors and Ascension Trust are responsible
> for assessing the risk to street pastors, and for taking
> any measures they consider necessary to mitigate the
> risks identified. They may ask the Metropolitan Police
> Service (MPS) for de-personalised information to assist
> in the risk assessment process. The MPS will respond to
> any calls for assistance by street pastors as urgently as
> circumstances allow.
>
> *Extract from the Draft Agreement*

Obviously, the police and the Home Office were watching and waiting to see what Street Pastors could do to bring reassurance to communities. Some still believed that we would be a liability and, naturally, they had to ask big questions about something with no track record. It was hard work! They always had more questions than we had answers. I had no idea I would have to jump through so many hoops just to get guns off the streets! It was all about slowly building trust. I remember at the time acknowledging that it was going to be a long, drawn-out process, particularly to iron out the legal implications and to consult with police solicitors and Home Office solicitors. However, in the end, the length of time it took— less than a year—was considered a very short time to have had such a document sanctioned at the highest levels.

> The concept began to intrigue me. I couldn't understand
> how an ordinary person like a street pastor could chat to
> a drug dealer late at night in an area with a high level of
> drug dealing. I remember watching on the CCTV screens

back at the station as street pastors approached dealers. They knelt down with one man and started praying. I
couldn't believe that. The computer aided dispatch (CAD)
staff in the control room were all glued to the CCTV
screen: they couldn't believe their eyes either.

Chief Inspector Sean Wilson

A mechanism of trust

The Agreement between the Met and Ascension Trust to facilitate the
safe surrender of firearms, drugs and offensive weapons was, if you
like, a shortcut to getting the support of other boroughs in London
(and beyond) because it made a great difference to how seriously they
viewed us. It went on to become a template that was used in each of the
forty-four police authorities in England and Wales.[9] Now, in the wider
context in which we are working, the Agreement means that Street
Pastors teams, wherever they are, don't have to reinvent the wheel, as
from this protocol they draw out their standard operational procedure.

The Agreement represented a massive show of confidence in the
Street Pastors initiative. It meant that the Met and the Home Office
believed that we were doing something good, for which they wanted
to create structures and policies that would help us to work. It was
an endorsement that police officers would take note of, and it gave
us more legitimacy to operate on the ground. This was a service-level
agreement, establishing a key relationship. Some officers in the middle
echelons of the force and some on the beat were still sceptical about us,

---

9   Until the national protocol agreement was made, the first agreement had to be tweaked slightly for use by other forces.

but again, it would take time for credibility to build. As crime figures went down where street pastors were on patrol, the 'softer' skills of street pastors were realised and a status quo was reached.

Within a year we were having conversations with the Met about a national protocol agreement. We met Street Pastors coordinators at a meeting in Birmingham, where we heard a senior police officer say that in all his years of policing this was the most satisfying piece of work he had ever been involved in. The Association of Chief Police Officers (ACPO) also sanctioned it. Two years ago we were asked if the Agreement could be used as the national protocol for other faith-based groups. This document, which we went on to develop, uses broader language so that, from a police perspective, it can cover other organisations. Now we have more enquiries from the police around the country about starting Street Pastors than we do from church leaders![10]

Personally speaking, our journey towards the Agreement with the police enabled me to see the police as a force for good. As a young black kid my experience of the police had not been good. I grew up thinking that I couldn't trust anyone in a uniform. Now I was seeing officers who were passionate about their jobs and who wanted to dedicate their professional skills to the betterment of communities.

I'm pleased to have been part of a movement of Christ, supporting the foundations of Street Pastors with more

---

10 The Street Pastors programme was recommended in *The Job*, the magazine of the Metropolitan Police, in an article describing a Safer Neighbourhoods Faith Forum, to encourage police officers to look at ways of expanding their Street Pastors schemes. 'Because of its proven success,' says the article, 'the Met is investing in expanding Street Pastors' coverage and development, including the introduction of School Pastors, who will provide a similar service, but focused on school travel routes.' *The Job*, December 2008, p. 5. Available at www.met.police.uk/job/job1001/the_job_31

than my prayers, and I cannot believe the reach the
initiative has across the UK and abroad. The interesting
dynamic for me is that it started as an initiative for black
and minority Christian communities and has developed
across culture and race to have street pastors of diverse
ethnicities and heritage. I never saw that coming, which
just shows you, when Christ is in charge, He brings communities together.

Bob Pull, former police inspector

Surrender your weapons

The first gun was surrendered in Birmingham in 2005. Street pastors
were approached by a young man who told us that he had been
carrying a gun around, with bullets that a friend had given him, and
that he felt trapped in that lifestyle. He was afraid to hand the gun
in to the police. We were the halfway house for that man. The senior
street pastor in the team contacted the police, telling them that we
had contact with this person and that a weapon was going to be
handed in. The gun was then collected and put into a safe in a church
and the police collected it from there. We counselled the young man,
directed him to a solicitor and were able to save massive amounts of
police time and effort. We were able to act as conduits, not wading in
but keeping our distance where appropriate. Weapons have also been
handed in to street pastors in Southend and Hackney.[11]

---

11 The surrender of weapons to street pastors is not widely publicised. As John Cheek, press and publicity officer for Southend
Street Pastors, observes, such stories may be wrongly reported, giving the impression that Street Pastors work more closely
with the police than they actually do. This could lead to a potential erosion of trust between Street Pastors and those they
meet on the streets, and could also increase the risk of possible confrontation.

There are many ways in which weapon surrender can happen. Conversations with street pastors could help someone there and then, or at a point in the future, to realise that they shouldn't carry a weapon. Street pastors provide an opportunity for a person in possession of a weapon to talk or think about their choice, and the opportunity for another course of action to be suggested. Measuring the quantity of weapons surrendered is not the best way to measure the value of this part of our role. It is important that we can be another option that is available to people, rather than them having no options at all. Even for a few incidences of surrender, the protocol for dealing with the possession of weapons, firearms or drugs will have been worth the effort.

> After the Southend team had been up and running for a year or so, a female volunteer was approached by someone who trusted the Street Pastors, and wanted her to pass on information to the police about the location of a gun. This individual was concerned that the gun should be recovered but didn't want Essex Police to know their identity. The address of the premises was discreetly passed on, and subsequently an armed weapon was removed and no questions were asked; the police were only too happy to accept the assistance given to them in the matter.
>
> Two potentially lethal knives have also been forwarded by Southend Street Pastors to the local constabulary. In one instance, a person arrived at the office we use as

our base and gave us a knife to hand in to the police.
On another occasion, an anonymous individual disclosed
to a member of the team the location of a blade hidden
in a bush nearby. The street pastor searched for it and
indeed, the knife had been secreted there, its where-
abouts probably only known about by a few people who
may have chosen to retrieve it and use it for nefarious
purposes at a later date. It too was quietly handed over.

Street pastor, Southend

The protocol has stood us in good stead. This was made very clear to me the night I took a call at home from a parent in a suburban area where we didn't have an agreement with the police. This parent had found a bag of drugs in his son's bedroom. It was a Saturday afternoon, but the father told me that he was very distressed and that he and his wife wanted to talk to me. I spent three hours with the parents that day. We talked about the implications of the son not being able to pay the dealer, and I advised them that they should find the money and give it to the son so that he could avoid the serious consequences of not paying. I left them in the early evening, taking the drugs with me.

So, picture the scene: there I was, outside the areas where we had a protocol agreement, with a bag of skunk weed. Imagine me explaining to officers that I was a reverend, and yes, that is a bag of drugs in the boot of my car. What I did was to phone one of the officers I had been dealing with in Lambeth before driving away from the house, so that the time and location of that call was logged on my phone and his. Then as I drove back into London, I had one of the most intimate prayer meetings I have ever had with the Lord! It was a tense drive back towards Lambeth, with me praying all the way. I let out an almighty 'hallelujah' when I crossed into the borough of Lambeth.

I was unable to get hold of our contact inspector, who was off-duty from Friday to Sunday, so I was forced to leave the drugs securely in the drawer of my office desk over the weekend![12] Having logged my phone call onto his phone, I felt reasonably happy to do this. I can't tell you how that office smelt when I came back in on Monday morning! If a police dog had come in it would have bounced off the ceiling! I was able that day to hand it in to nearby Brixton police station with help of the officer at Lambeth. It took nearly an hour to get through the paperwork (and that was the short version)!

A complementary relationship

The very first patrol by Taunton Street Pastors was commended for assisting in the restoration of a stolen handbag to its owner. The team encountered a young man running down a side street holding a woman's handbag and decided to monitor his progress, presuming that he was up to no good.

The chap stopped a little way along the street, enabling the Street Pastors team to catch up with him and ask what was going on. It transpired that far from being

---

12 Each Street Pastors team has a duty sergeant, inspector or superintendent to whom they report.

of criminal intent, he had intercepted a grab-and-run crime by three young thieves on the town bridge. He had wrestled the handbag from the miscreants and had given chase but been outrun and was unable to apprehend them. The young man explained that he had been unable to find the owner and had set off again to look for the thieves. When asked what he was planning to do with the handbag he said that he was minded to take the bag home and look through the contents to try and identify and contact the owner the next morning.

The street pastors sensitively advised him that his proposed course of action was not the best way to conclude what had hitherto been a commendable response. On this occasion the senior street pastor had been entrusted with the mobile phone number of the duty police sergeant and so was able to contact the sergeant direct and request a police attendance quickly. There followed a brief moment of uncertainty as the police asked the closed circuit television operators to review the recording by the cameras trained on the town bridge. The cameras were not covering the bridge throughout the period of the crime and so only showed the young woman and the man who had retrieved the handbag from the snatchers. For a moment the police were about to arrest him for seizing the bag, but the street pastors remonstrated and asked that his story be heard fully.

> By this time the young woman had independently
> reported the crime and was in another police vehicle,
> which was heading back to the scene to enable her
> to corroborate the story given by the young man. The
> police were suitably impressed when he reunited the bag
> with its contacts intact with its shaken but very grateful
> owner. The police took the young lady for a drive through
> the town centre where, remarkably, she was able to iden-
> tify the young men.
>
> *Street pastor, Taunton*

When the police respond to a situation, they do so in order to detect or apprehend or restore order. In contrast, a street pastor's job is to care and listen. We can do things that the police don't have time for; they can do things we can't. It's complementary.

Street Pastors senior coordinator in South Manchester, Tony Winter, is also a member of a Divisional Independent Advisory Group (IAG) in Greater Manchester, with responsibility for policing and youth policy.[13] In this capacity his job is to lessen the impact of the police's role in sensitive communities. Where there is a serious crime issue relating to a young person, Tony will be invited along to keep relations peaceful. Tony tells the story of how on one occasion he was invited to accompany the police on a raid on a house where a suspect lived. The police broke the door down, the suspect's mother was screaming abuse from inside and children were crying. The police told her they had a member of the IAG with them, and she

---

13 I am grateful to Tony Winter for talking to me about various issues raised in this book.

could speak to him if she wished. 'I don't care about any IAG,' came back the reply. Then the officers said, 'It's Tony the street pastor,' and she opened the door and he was able to talk to her.

Some Street Pastors teams have been blessed with support from the Christian Police Association (CPA). In Torbay, Street Pastors coordinators were invited to give a talk at the CPA's carol service at the Devon and Cornwall Police Headquarters. They went in their uniforms and, after the service, got talking to the chief constable. He expressed an interest in supporting the Street Pastors team, and when the time came for the commissioning service for street pastors in Torbay, the chief constable put the coordinators in touch with Chris Singer, superintendent for Torbay policing, a Christian officer. Now the whole team has regular quarterly meetings with the superintendent, with the freedom to tell him how their relationship with the police is working or how it could be improved.

Although members of the CPA can help to bring Street Pastors to the notice of their senior officers, the decision to work with Street Pastors is always made by senior officers. Often those senior officers prefer not to appoint a Christian officer to lead the relationship between the force and the Street Pastors team, and so most officers we deal with do not profess a Christian faith. I think this is healthy. We are not seeking alliances only with Christians, but with men and women who are interested in what we can do and who know that we can bring added value to the community.

Places of safety

On the television, whether it be a news programme or *Traffic Cops*, we get glimpses of the force undertaking the long and complicated business of bringing justice to criminals. The streets are an important arena for the police. It is where we, the public, see them responding to problems; it is where we want to find them accessible, visible and approachable. Your town will have a dedicated neighbourhood safety team, but there remains a significant role for volunteers, because the police can't build safer communities on their own, nor should they. Police value the presence of Street Pastors teams, who are available to create moments of safety for people who are at their most vulnerable. Street pastors can give time to the people they meet. After all, the phone will not be demanding their attention in the early hours; there will be no meeting to go to, no email to respond to. There are many, many stories of the small ways in which street pastors have met the needs of people on the streets. One email, 'From a grateful parent', tells of the difference a street pastor made to one boy and his family.

To whom it may concern,

Just a short message to say thank you very much to the street pastor who brought my son home safely last night. It's the first time he has been drunk and he is now slowly recovering, licking his wounds! I dread to think what would have happened to him if the street pastor wasn't there.

I thank you again and keep up the good work. The street pastors are a good help to the many youngsters (or

adults) who need help in bad situations. Let's hope that
it will be a lesson to my lad and next time he will think
wisely.

Partnership working has been a significant step for the police, as
well as for Ascension Trust. The recognition that the battle against
crime would not be won by enforcement only in a place such as
Brixton has produced a vital sea-change in policing, and I hope that
we have helped to move that debate along. It is only regeneration
that has made an impact on the climate of fear that exists in some
areas or the antagonism police experience towards policies like Stop
and Search, and Christians are increasingly playing their part in the
regeneration of communities.

I don't know what the psychology is, but when we brought
in street cleaners to tidy up an area, the drug dealers
moved away; they didn't like dealing in clean areas.
When there is something visibly wrong in a community,
such as excessive litter, blatant drug dealing, burned-
out cars, damaged windows, something far greater
than these things in themselves is going on. An environment is created in which criminality feels comfortable.
Ultimately it is not just the graffiti or the litter that defines
the environment: people become the environment which
they themselves have created or allowed to be created.
In the end the community becomes conditioned by the
environment. It is this cycle that needs to be broken.

Chief Inspector Sean Wilson

Though it may be for different reasons, Street Pastors and the police want to achieve the same end. Our relationship with the police, their involvement in the training of street pastors and the many other ways in which they are assisting teams to get out into communities safely and responsibly are all helping to alter the balance of power in our towns and cities.

CHAPTER EIGHT

THE SLEEPING GIANT
The Voice, 27 January 2003

The church in action: bringing clarity

The story of the birth and growth of the initiative is the story of the church working in alliance with the power structures in our communities. However, at the heart of the work of Street Pastors is the stipulation that a Street Pastors team is not resourced by one church alone, but by several, and so the story of Street Pastors is also the story of churches working with each other, and the journey towards an interdenominational church response. One of the obvious hallmarks of Street Pastors—before you mention crime rates, or lives changed—is that the initiative has brought the church together at a grassroots level in a very significant way. Yet like many other ecumenical initiatives, it has had to overcome theological and traditional boundaries between denominations.

Even though the gospel is at the heart of why we do what we do, it is not at the forefront of what we say. As a result, because street

pastors do not go out to preach the gospel as such, theological differences haven't carried the weight that they do in many ecumenical
projects. Even so, I still find that, sadly, this part of the Street Pastors
story contains some unpalatable aspects of church life.

Partnership problems

The Street Pastors initiative is designed to help Christians be bridge-
builders in today's society. When we are truly communicating with
someone, we turn something complex into something simple. This
can happen person-to-person or be facilitated by one person on
behalf of another, for instance, in relation to a local government
department, healthcare services, a community project, or a returning-
to-education course. The bottom line is that people who are able to
give connect with people who need to *receive*, and in the same way,
bridges sometimes need to be built from church to church as well.

As I set up the Street Pastors scheme I realised to a greater extent
than I had previously that there was fragmentation among churches
and, in some places, mistrust of the Churches Together initiative.
There was also uncertainty surrounding the churches' collaboration
with other agencies, such as local government departments and the
police. I have always argued that we are more effective in represent-
ing the message of Jesus when we build bridges between the church
and political, social, civic and community groups. However, in
establishing the initiative I met considerable criticism of the 'urban
trinity' concept; criticism that appeared from slightly different angles
depending on which denomination I talked to.[1]

---

1   For more on the 'urban trinity' see chapter 5.

From the evangelical side of the British church, I was told that Street Pastors 'polluted' Christianity and damaged its distinctiveness, because I advocated partnership with the police and other agencies. However, I have never claimed that our Christian identity—manifest in the power and grace of our Lord Jesus—is untouchable or never at risk of being tarnished. Christians all over the world live with the challenge to be distinctively Christian in secular societies; to take responsibility for the world, but not become like it, to be 'in it' but not 'of it' (among many verses, see Rom. 12:2; John 17:15; 2 Cor. 10:3). We have to negotiate this relationship all the time, being alert to compromise but being ready to get our hands dirty. David Shosanya dissects the relationship between denominations and other agencies in this country in the following way:

> The white Baptist church has a mistrust of working with partners outside of the church because of its history of dissent; it is more concerned about freedom of choice, based on conscience. Its birth in the split from the Church of England has led to a mistrust of institutions. African and Caribbean churches are wary of working with non-church agencies because of a power disparity. African and Caribbean Christians have come into this country but have not known how to interpret the power structure or play their part in it. They may think that an institution such as Social Services has some kind of intelligence-gathering function, and may be involved in covert surveillance (a manifestation of racism).

Church of England people are happy to interact with
statutory agencies and, in fact, feel they are a part of
them. Charismatic or 'new' church groups are sometimes
suspicious of other agencies because they question
whether there is a genuine willingness to interact with
them at a level that is dignifying. They think they might
be approached in a paternalistic way. Plus their spiritual
descriptions of 'salt and light', and their awareness of the
Holy Spirit speaking, clash with the institutional rhetoric
they come up against and this leads to frustration and
mistrust.

'For some churches,' David continues, 'where ministries similar to Street Pastors have been going on for years, reluctance to
join with us may indicate that offence has been taken because
this relatively new, branded initiative has eclipsed their own.' In
general terms there has been an absence of support, or a lack of an
equivocal response, from black church leaders for Street Pastors.
They don't see why they should do something that is already in
their 'portfolio' under the umbrella of a particular brand. To
Ascension Trust, David has therefore posed the question, 'What
strategies has the Trust used to develop its relationships with these
churches?' For church leaders from the African and Caribbean
communities, we know that a phone call or a letter does not
work. Sandwiches do not work, either; you've got to take them
for a proper meal! We may need to ask more questions of our own
part in these relationships.

Which church are you from?

Working to establish the Street Pastors initiative helped me to see that people outside the church perceive it to be divided. Nearly every time I go out on the streets as a street pastor I am asked, 'Which church are you from?' I always reply, 'All of them.' Sadly, the fact that this question is asked tells me that many people hold the idea that 'church' is a fragmented institution, that there are too many denominations, and all you can get from it is a good dose of confusion about what Christians stand for.

Ironically, we don't often preach doctrine, but we *separate* ourselves with doctrine. Yet the world is saying, 'I want to see your faith in action.' People are broken; they don't care about the niceties of what we believe. They are saying, 'Can you help me?'

> A journalist from *Community Care* magazine asked me why the church was sending out street pastors, and I said Jesus called us to care for those in need and go out with the Good News. I compared the church to a dung heap—smelly if kept in one place but it does a power of good when spread around to fertilise the garden. Jesus put it more felicitously; he called us to be salt and light.
>
> *Street pastor, Sutton*

If ever it was clear to me that the church is divided on theological lines, traditional lines and racial lines, it was when I began to think through the importance of the Street Pastors initiative being a church response, rather than a racial or cultural or denominational response. However, I have never been naïve about the difficulties of achieving this. I met once with one of the officers under Sir John Stevens, the Metropolitan Police commissioner from 2000 to 2005. He came to see me to talk about Sir John's vision for working with the churches. I remember the officer saying that one of Sir John's visions was to get the churches together. I paused for a moment and then replied to the officer that Sir John was rather ambitious, because Jesus has been trying for two thousand years to unite his church and he hasn't been successful yet!

I have met people up and down the country who have strong reservations about working with other denominations. These views will not deal with the problems out on the streets and in our communities. What will bring about change is, according to Scripture, 'if my people, who are called by my name, will humble themselves and pray and seek my face … then I will heal their land' (2 Chron. 7:14). We need to shake our priorities up. If we held less tightly to our theological views, we might be better able to look around us and recognise that our society is decaying, both spiritually and morally. Therefore, our priorities should be to bring clarity and to bring people together in order to help our society discover what it means to be whole in every sense.

I have heard statements like this: 'If the Catholics are involved, I'm not going to be in it.' Ironically, many in the Catholic Church are still looking cautiously over the fence at Street Pastors. We would love to be working with them—they have so much to offer. We have all come across prejudices about the way people 'do church', whether they raise their hands, pray for the sick, or speak in tongues. Some Christians need to know what will happen next in a service; they want an order of service, with no surprises. Others prefer spontaneity in worship and an unpredictable service format. I have always found it helpful, if challenging, to get stuck into the traditional, ceremonial differences between denominations—just go along with whatever is happening and get some firsthand experience of another way of worshipping.

I remember the first invitation I received to preach at an Anglican church. Coming from a Pentecostal and charismatic background as I did, it was bound to be a culture shock! To begin with I was offered a robe to wear. I then walked through the building in procession, amidst all the bells and smells, and once the service had started, I began to navigate my way through the order of service, losing my place several times. I had ten minutes to preach, instead of the forty-five I was used to. That particular day it was a communion service, which, of course, I wanted to be part of. As I knelt at the altar rail, I was shocked when the priest blessed me on the head and moved on! I looked up and caught his eye, as if to say 'What about me?' I realised I had to put my hands out to receive the communion wafer. Then the chalice came along. I made sure I was giving off all the right body language to get my share, but got more than I bargained for and was nearly knocked out by the strength of the wine! Afterwards an elderly lady said to me, 'Young man, I thought your preaching was excellent this morning. It is the first time I have stayed awake in church for several years!'

There are many differences to overcome. I'm sure God smiles at us as he constantly challenges us to get on with what we need to do. When we work together His will is done on earth as it is in heaven, and communities will be revived and transformed.

Within some Christian communities in some of our towns and cities, the idea of Churches Together is not popular. There is some cynicism about the word *ecumenical*: it has got mixed-up with multi-faith. Yet the book of Psalms says how 'good and pleasant it is when brothers live together in unity!' (Ps. 133:1). Many of us have grown up with in-built prejudices about different parts of the church and how they operate. I'd like us all to say, 'Yes, we do things differently, but we are passionate about Jesus, His grace and His mercy.'

> Yet even in our small town, some of the Christians did not know each other, and getting Christians together has been a wonderful spin-off from Street Pastors. Prayer times have been really special; I see Street Pastors as a forum for people to pray together across the churches. Street Pastors is the main focus, but it has had the effect of drawing people together. Our prayer coordinator has tried to incorporate different models of prayer to bring all our traditions together so that everyone feels they can participate.
>
> *Street pastor, Heathfield*

What is evident within our nation and communities is that we have fraternities of ministers (mainstream or independent churches) operating within their own paradigms. Not enough of them are taking the time to cross-fertilise and build relationships with other communities and denominations. It has been very obvious in the UK that because of the lack of that deep cooperation between church leaders, there are many issues and challenges in communities about which the church does not really have a strong voice to represent itself. Church leaders need to recognise that these links can take place on a variety of levels. Some people are comfortable with committees; in other contexts, people can come together as part of a 'deanery'. For example, I serve as the ecumenical borough dean in Lambeth. This is something that was started by Anglicans and Catholics but is now open to other traditions. For others, having a meal together or meeting together for prayer is the most appropriate thing.

Never underestimate the power of relationship! It helps people to understand different views, worldviews and theological views. The acceptance and understanding of those views grow out of strong relationships. What I see as I travel around the country is that, although congregations may have existed in a place for years, ministers have never had time to build relationships with others. At times of real need in their community they are unable to give a robust response to the challenge. I believe these things are a hindrance to the church engaging effectively with our communities today. I'd like to pose the question, 'What could interchurch relationships look like in your setting?'

What does unity look like?

The church in this country has, I feel, been part of an unproductive loop, in which Christians look around them and conclude that other Christians are slightly wacky; non-Christians think we are *all* wacky, and while we are all wrapped up in this, the world is going down the pan! One of the things that the Lord is doing through Street Pastors is helping the crossover between theological and traditional boundaries to happen.

I strongly believe that no one denomination or stream of church can deal with or respond to the problems and challenges that we are facing today in the twenty-first century. They are mammoth. We need to respond from a church perspective that reflects and represents the history of skills, expertise, insight and resources—all the things that make us uniquely able to respond to the deep social, economic and spiritual challenges of our time.

When I think of the Catholic Church and the many good works that it has done over the years, I am truly encouraged. Likewise the Anglicans and various other mainstream churches. The amount of good work we have all done, whether short-term or long-term, has been phenomenal. Then I think about the African and Caribbean community, and the work that they are doing in terms of Saturday schools, supplementary education (much of it largely unnoticed), and I always come to the same conclusion: imagine what the impact would be if there was collective thinking and a joined-up strategy? If that was happening, how much more could we impact communities?

One of the best models that I have seen of churches complementing and helping each other was in Jamaica, and chapter 4 has described how instructive this was to me. At least 90 percent of the membership of Bruce Fletcher's uptown church were influential, highly educated people, but they not only had a worldview of Christianity, they saw the needs in other parts of their city. So the affluent church, together with others like it, drew alongside the downtown church, which was struggling in an area of deprivation, poverty and high crime. So in this context, here was a church saying that it wanted to take its expertise to help the church downtown and attempt to understand the problems it faced and the problems its neighbourhood faced.

> Perhaps the most striking and challenging aspect of the Trench Town experience is the dynamic between Pastors Wilmot and Fletcher. Revd Fletcher pastors an affluent uptown church in Kingston. He and his congregation felt a burden for the deprived area of their city. However, instead of simply sending evangelism teams into those areas of deprivation, Pastor Fletcher felt God leading him to partner with local pastors already established within the areas of need. Obediently, Pastor Fletcher's church began to work with and support the work of Pastor Wilmot in Trench Town. The result, a union that powerfully demonstrates the effectiveness of co-operation between affluent and financially challenged congregations.
>
> 'Can anything good come out of Trench Town?'
>
> Candlelight, *June 2002*

The group of uptown churches did some social analysis to find out the needs of the downtown area in order to help the church there engage with its community and to empower people in terms of opportunity and education. Not only did they do this analysis, they invested money and people skills into those communities. This is a good example, a biblical example, of a church recognising that its neighbour is not just the person who lives nearby, nor is it only someone who lives on the other side of the world, but it can also be someone who lives in another part of their city.

When Street Pastors started work in Manchester, in the Inner South area of the city, it was extremely difficult to get the churches outside that community to see that the Inner South area was struggling to cope with its problems. Some places had acute problems and needed the wider church to meet with their brothers and sisters and ask, 'How can we serve you best so that you are able to respond to the challenges you are facing?' Likewise, churches like those in the Manchester Inner South district needed to have the confidence to ask for help. Again, if the church acknowledged a call to respond together, we could have a powerful response with a significant impact.

Street Pastors has facilitated this interdependence by stipulating that a minimum of four different denominations must work together to bring Street Pastors to a community. If you are serious about Street Pastors, you can't do it on your own. Some churches have said they are ready to start Street Pastors with seventy people from their own congregation. We have had to say, 'No thanks ... find some other churches.' Even if a church had a thousand people available the initiative would not be a true reflection of the body of Christ, and it would be less likely to have the longevity we aim for. One church with a group of people ready to be involved in Street Pastors but wanting to do it on their own does not model anything except willingness to be involved. Running projects independently may mean that churches miss out on financial assistance, and they will certainly miss out on the refreshment that other churches can bring.

I want churches to develop strategy together, to reason together, to look at the needs of their community together. There is a practical logic in this for, as the Bible says, 'one man chase[s] a thousand, or two put ten thousand to flight' (Deut. 32:30). This makes biblical and business sense. Our impact can be so much greater. In some areas twenty-seven churches are working together! They have never had that unity there before.

Reclaiming public space

Street Pastors has helped people to recapture a historic vision about the church in the public space, or in spaces that are contested. David Shosanya explains the distance between churches and communities, or the lack of relevance of the one for the other, as a result of the British church's 'gentrification'.

> The church in this country has always had a problem with reaching working class people (or, non-middle class people). I see the Street Pastors initiative as offering a bridge to these groups. It demonstrates one way that an ordinary Christian can be that bridge. It says, 'You can do it, without being anything other than you already are.'

> The white middle classes have always felt protective of their communities, but this has been lost through the fragmentation and increased mobility of our modern lives. Street Pastors allows us to build relationships from grass roots and allows Christians to rediscover the connections with other people that have been lost.

Releasing local Christians into ministry

In 2004, as Street Pastors in the borough of Lewisham was taking root, the coordinator Eustace Constance received a number of messages from a long-distance lorry driver who was longing to be a street pastor. It was difficult to arrange a meeting with him, but when the two eventually met, it happened to be in the same week that Eustace had met a church leader to whom he had presented the work of Street Pastors. The minister had responded by saying that she didn't believe that she had anyone in her church who would be interested. The church was busy with cubs and scouts, raising funds for the church roof, and many other things. The minister expressed concerns about the safety of Street Pastors but wished us well. Eustace had asked for the opportunity to share the initiative more widely with the congregation at that church, but the minister spoke confidently on behalf of her flock. When Eustace met the lorry driver later that week, with whom he had a long and invigorating conversation about Street Pastors, guess which church he belonged to? 'You really need to meet with my minister!' the man said. 'She would love this!' He was wrong about her, and she was wrong about him!

We place great importance on our relationships with churches; Street Pastors can't happen without that relationship. To be accepted onto the training course, a volunteer must be committed to a local church. Yet in some cases Street Pastors may pose a challenge to church leaders, not least because it might draw people away from the ministries the church is already running. Based on the truism that 20 percent of Christians do 80 percent of the work in churches, Street Pastors probably draws from that small pool of activists. There may some-times be a corresponding problem, that a church will lose finances if people redirect their time and resources into a project other than the 'in-house' one. There is a natural conflict of interest, but leaders need to cast a broader vision that encourages people to access different initiatives and use different skills. In one sense, the vision that they shape will then go on to be about what those individuals bring back to the church and the opportunities for enrichment, diversity and focus that are embedded in them.

Within many congregations members have a strong desire to respond to the climate of our society. There are people who don't see themselves as a preacher, a deacon, a leader, but know that there is something they need to do to earth their Christianity. Some churches may have plenty of their own projects, while others lack any strategy for involvement in their communities, but are blessed with individuals who have a heart for people. Hence our prayer is that we will reach the one or two people in a church who are ready and waiting for Street Pastors. We say to church leaders, 'You may not have a project that can release people, but we have.'

If the church can't do it …

I believe that parachurch organisations, like Ascension Trust, should exist alongside churches. Some churches, however, don't want to be in relationship with parachurch movements, and it is equally true that some parachurch groups work too independently of churches. Parachurch organisations need to have a sense of reliance on church members, just as churches need to know that sometimes their members are looking for a channel to express their faith that is outside of the church organisation. Parachurch groups are not constrained by the same structures as churches, although they should be accountable to church leadership teams. In my experience, the church needs them to help sharpen people and provide an outlet that will benefit many of their members.

Projects that are shaped and delivered by churches themselves do mobilise Christians, so of course they are good. Yet all the benefits of any one project, I believe, are outweighed when Christians work together for the benefit of the community. We can so easily get blinkered. My desire is that people don't get carried away with Street Pastors, but that they get carried away with the church! That they begin to get a revelation of the body of Christ, an army of different parts moving together. When we go to church we go to the place of our faithfulness, the place of our learning and discipleship, the place where we encourage one another. Meeting together like this is one of the forms of obedience that God calls us to. But we should not proclaim the reality of our institutions—we proclaim the principles of God's kingdom and his love for us in Jesus. Street Pastors is the church in action.

As an interchurch effort, Street Pastors is the body of Christ saying we are taking responsibility for our community.

> In terms of mission practice in England, it is this that makes Street Pastors one of the most credible initiatives. For as we read in the Gospel of John, it is by loving each other that we model God's love for us—'by this all men will know that you are my disciples' (John 13:35).
>
> *David Shosanya*

Ecumenism used to be about tea and biscuits. Reverend Dr Pat Took, regional minister team leader for the London Baptist Association, has called Street Pastors 'the new ecumenism'.

When churches work together, this models the priorities for the Christian gospel. What difference does this unity make to the person on the street? David Shosanya gives the following assessment:

> It counteracts people's natural inclination to think that religion is divisive. It shows that there is sufficient common ground between many different people that they can come together under this banner to make a difference to the locality. Everybody is out there under one mission statement and they are putting their differences aside. People are more religiously literate than we think. When they see us together it is a realisation of their unconscious hopes for the church. 'I wonder if there is a God?' they think. 'Perhaps the fact that Christians get on well means that there is.'

Therefore I see a redemptive component in Street Pastors, because it changes the way people see the church and the community. People outside our churches are conscious that Christians have the potential to be a voice that is listened to. 'If the church can't do it,' they think, 'we are scuppered.'

CHAPTER NINE

BRINGING PRAYER TO THE MEAN STREETS
The Times, 4 October 2008

First steps

Our first outing as a team took place in April 2003, accompanied by a BBC cameraman. We met at Ascension Trust headquarters in Brixton and prayed together. There were eighteen of us on that first night. There were two church leaders, a medical student and several single mums. I was shocked to see that there were only three men, of which I was one! My conclusion was that the men were at home doing the mental risk assessment! In contrast the women, with their maternal instinct, decided that they needed to get out there. I know that many of them felt that it could be their son or grandson on the streets. I was very moved by that. There were so many men in church leadership, yet it was women who came forward to face this challenge. This ratio stayed the same for the first three years, then in the fourth year more men started to get involved.

I wondered how people would respond to us and remembered those people interviewed by *The Voice* newspaper who said we should stay at home or in our churches. We might be ignored; we might have a negative experience. Would we be welcomed? What happened if something went wrong? All these things played on my mind and did battle with the tremendous sense of occasion that I was also feeling as I said to myself, 'This is it!' Jesus has called us to be the light of the world, to shine light into the darkness, to bring peace in turmoil and hope where there is hopelessness! We had to find out what kind of experience God had in store for us.

As we walked we introduced ourselves to everyone—doormen, shop owners, pub landlords. When we reached the main road in Brixton, we separated into two teams. A police vehicle sped past and then turned round and pulled alongside us. The officer at the wheel was full of praise for us; he had seen something on TV and wanted to affirm us. Wow! Next we met a woman on the streets. I greeted her and introduced ourselves, told her what we were doing and why we were doing it. 'Do you think that is a good idea?' I asked her. 'Yes, I will feel safer walking home at night knowing you are out here,' was her reply.

We went through several estates where groups of young people were hanging out. We could see that one group was watching us. After a while it looked as if they were getting ready to move away, but then one of them called over, 'Street Pastors? Who are you? Why are you doing this?' That was all we needed for several conversations to spring up. Our uniform grabbed people's attention and made them ask who we were. We walked on and another car drove past, did a U-turn and came back to us. 'Who are you people?' the driver asked, leaning out of the window. I talked to him about the problems on our streets and why the church needs to get out and engage with troubled communities. I asked him what he thought about young people carrying guns and was startled by his reply. 'I carry a gun,' he said, pointing to the glove compartment. 'If I didn't, people would take advantage of me. I've even given my mother a can of CS gas to spray in case she is attacked.' I was amazed at the ease with which he told me this. He was simply saying, 'This is the way things are.' He ended with the challenge, 'You've got a big job on your hands.' He doubted that we would be able to deal with this problem.

Alison Lievesley and Marilyn Garber were in the team of street pastors that night.

The thing that stood out most for me that night was how willing people were to talk to us. We'd taken a route through the estates and chatted with various people of many ages before we bumped into a woman who was heading home for the night. There was nothing particularly insightful about our conversation, but maybe she just needed to talk. Maybe we seemed safe, or maybe she simply hadn't spoken to anyone in a while, but a story poured out about her son who had been killed on the streets. We listened, we offered what comfort we could with our presence, and we asked if she'd like us to pray for her—and she said yes. And she wasn't the only one. I've been in situations where people have agreed to prayer instantly because they want to meet

Jesus and be healed, but I honestly never thought I'd see someone that ready to be prayed for on the streets of this country. And yet on that first night out everyone we spoke to wanted prayer as much as they wanted to talk.

Alison Lievesley

Our first night out was a thrilling experience. None of us knew what to really expect and we were all filled with anticipation. Not fear, but eager anticipation as to who we would meet, what we would do, how we would be received and the impact we would make. When we were out there we were received very well, although some people were uncertain as to who we were, and we even got asked if we were dustbin men!

One of the encounters that has stayed with me from that first night out was meeting a young lady along Mare Street. This lady was in her late teens and she was pushing a pram. It was very early in the morning and not the time you would expect to see a mum and baby out in the street. This young lady explained to us that she was a first-time mum and that her baby was crying and she didn't know what to do so she thought she would take the child out. This was a really golden moment as we were able to give support and encouragement to this young mum. By being on the street that night God used us to bring guidance, strengthening and affirmation to that young lady.

After praying with this young mum, we turned around to find a man standing next to us with a snake around his neck! This was another thing we didn't expect to see on the streets of Hackney in the early hours of the morning.

Marilyn Garber

The cameraman temporarily left us at this point because we knew we were heading for a district where drug dealers operated. As we walked around the corner we saw groups of dealers, maybe eight of them, spread out twenty-five metres apart. There was a fast trade, with people pulling up in their cars all the time. That first night, we said, 'Good evening', and most of them just looked up and grunted. However, one of the dealers said, 'Pastor, will you pray for me? I need prayer.' My heart raced. What do I pray for? Do I pray that the police lock him up tonight? Do I pray God's blessing on his entrepreneurial ventures? Silently, I prayed hard asking the Lord to give me the words. I thought to myself, this has got to be quite a creative prayer! I was just about to pray out loud when a man walked up to the dealer, obviously wanting drugs. The dealer said to him, 'Go away. I'm having the pastor pray for me ... Not now!' Then I prayed for God's help for this man, to give him a sense of purpose and lead him in a path of righteousness. He said a loud 'Amen' and sincerely thanked me for my prayers.

As time went by we were gradually able to develop a relationship with the dealers on this patch. The second week that we passed that way we greeted the men again, saying 'Hi' and 'Good-night'. On the third week we started to have a few more conversations with them. One of them in particular opened up to me about his problems. It's difficult to know what to say to dealers. I have never said to them that they are doing something wrong, but generally when I'm talking with a dealer, they start to feel uncomfortable about what they are doing. They often feel they have to justify themselves.

In Brixton town centre, many people thanked us for being out on the streets, showing that we care. Many seemed more excited than we were that the church had left the building! One person asked us if we got paid for doing it, and when I told him that we didn't and, in fact, we had to pay for our own training and uniform, he happily used a few expletives! He couldn't get his head around it.

I was delighted that members of the public were so inquisitive. That first outing gave us so many insights into the community. I realised that we were seeing more than drugs and danger; we were seeing people living their lives and going about their business in the places that they lived. Particularly in summer months, the night time streets of South London are filled with people—just like daytime—with older folk bringing chairs out of their houses to sit and pass the time of day with their neighbours. We always like to greet people with a 'Good evening' or 'Hi there', because where communities are living with tension, people tend to mind their own business and avoid eye contact, looking straight ahead all the time. It is very important for us as street pastors to break the ice and engage people.

Lewisham

We started with only eighteen street pastors deployed in the two boroughs of Hackney and Lambeth. It felt very daunting to start work with a third borough, Lewisham, in 2004. The borough was probably the first place that made contact with us (rather than the other way around). Sergeant Tony Unthank of the Community Safety Team in Lewisham initiated the contact and arranged a meeting with his borough commander. As he presented the Street Pastors concept to the commander, he had no idea what kind of response he would get, but he was driven by a radical dream—to one day see more street pastors on the streets than police! Unusually, the local authority had already made clear its interest. Steve Bullock, mayor of Lewisham, came out with us early on and we were included in the borough's annual strategy for safety in 2003. Our work, and specifically the work of our first area coordinator, Eustace Constance, was to maintain this interest, improve relationships, and bring local churches on board. Using a directory of churches in the borough, Eustace tirelessly ploughed through many introductions over the phone and went to numerous face-to-face meetings. A few people had caught a whisper, but not many paid serious attention to us. We got used to hearing that we were naïve and that we were putting well-meaning people in danger. There was a lot of hard work to do to raise awareness and introduce the concept.

Birmingham

From this point we began to have a strong sense that we must reach the other major cities that were being affected by guns and drugs, most notably Birmingham and Manchester. When I went to Aston and Lozells in Birmingham as part of the 'Guns on our streets' tour, the church leaders in that area had not been convinced that Street Pastors would work. They had seen many initiatives come and go. Two leaders, however, Calvin Young and Sandra Thomas, were different. Pastor Young believed that the initiative was desperately needed in his community. I remember discussing with both Pastor Young and Pastor Thomas that it was important that church leaders owned the project. To be in a situation where we dropped an initiative into an area and maintained it long-distance was clearly a bad idea. It would only work if local churches were at the root of it.

My first port of call was to speak to the chairman of Churches Together in Aston and Lozells, and he asked for more time to think about our plans. I respected what that church leader had said, and in the end, those church leaders in Aston and Lozells still did not come on board. However, Pastors Young and Thomas put the full resources of their church behind us, and it was down to the convictions of those two pastors that it was possible for the initiative to be launched in Birmingham on 17 March 2004. Street pastors in Birmingham have found themselves in the middle of tense situations many times, but they have willingly responded and made a positive difference to community relationships.

> One night, the street pastors had no keys to get into the office. This meant briefing and prayer had to be done on the corner of the street ... not ideal, but in this case, clearly God's plan. As the street pastors prayed, they

heard a commotion across the street. A fight had broken out in a small backstreet club between a group of local Caribbean youths and some Somalian lads from another area. The team of four street pastors went straight into action and attempted to calm the situation. They not only broke up the fight, but when the Caribbean youths had run off, they called the police and subsequently persuaded them to take the Somalian youths back across the city to save them from the backlash that had been threatened. In the waiting period, the team were able to calm the men and have a great conversation about why they were helping. Without street pastors, who knows what else would have happened between those two sets of youths?

Street pastor, Birmingham

The following year, Street Pastors teams were out in the Lozells area of the city at the time of the disturbances in October 2005, trying to bring calm between the riot police and their community. Following the riots, members of the team spent five days meeting with young Pakistani and Caribbean men, helping to diffuse the tension.

Manchester

During the 'Guns on our streets' tour there was so much that touched my mind and heart about Manchester. In fact, the tour helped to build momentum for a 'Gangstop' march which took place shortly afterwards in the summer of 2002, and tuned in to a desire among

local people to respond to the increasing levels of violence and shootings in the area.[1] What came out of the tour and other community
meetings was that there were many small projects in these areas of
deprivation, with everybody doing their own thing and working to
their own agendas. This is usually a situation that drains resources and
can lead to ineffectiveness. I was asked if I would convene a meeting
between the various community groups in the local sports club, a
place called The Powerhouse, and ultimately develop an umbrella
organisation for all the groups and charities that were working in the
area. A large crowd gathered on the evening of the meeting, among
which was MP Tony Lloyd and several local councillors.

As I opened the meeting, I reminded the audience of why I was
there and the sort of outcome we were looking for. I outlined a process to identify and set up an organisation to reflect the dynamics of
the community, speak on its behalf, facilitate the various different
organisations and publicise them to the wider public. Towards the
end I took a question from the floor: 'Why are you, someone who is
based in London, chairing this meeting?' Good question. I explained
that many people had asked me to come, and that I had come at
my own expense. 'Why had not a local church leader convened this
meeting?' the questioner continued. 'You need to go and ask them
that,' I replied. The non-attendance of church leaders at this meeting
was noted with some indignation by members of the public.

It was proposed that I should lead this process, and this was
seconded by Tony Lloyd MP. What did this mean for me? Could
I deliver the goods and come to Manchester and bring the process

---

1   For this picture of events in Inner South Manchester at this time I am grateful to Paul Keeble, and for his generosity in making
    his draft thesis, *Mission With*, available to me. See also www.carisma.me.uk.

to a successful conclusion? I travelled to Manchester several times over the next few months to chair a series of community meetings. Sharing this development with my church in London, one of the congregation—a retired businessman called Hugh Allen—volunteered to drive me to Manchester twice a month. We would leave early in the morning and be in Manchester by 9.30 a.m. The Lord provided for me through Hugh for a whole year. During that time I met Paul Keeble, a graduate from Manchester University who, together with his wife, Judith, had heard God's call to serve inner-city Manchester. Paul became the administrator for this process.

Where was Street Pastors in this? The organisation, now known as CARISMA (Community Alliance for Renewal, Inner South Manchester Area), wanted to get Street Pastors involved as part of its portfolio, but parallel to this was the need to coordinate the local groups. In the end we progressed the two 'arms' at the same time, and ultimately CARISMA facilitated Street Pastors in the area. We badly needed to get churches on board, but the context for Street Pastors was CARISMA, which was a community organisation, not a Christian one (although, as Paul Keeble points out, the majority of the initial core group would identify themselves as Christians).[2] So it was important that we acted democratically, met all the stakeholders and continued to help them to work together. We had to work through a lot of competing initiatives and hold together a group of people with different ideas.

Yet God is not just working through Street Pastors, and therefore we must be able to respond to and deal with a mosaic of people

---

2   Keeble, chapter 2, *CARISMA: History and Story So Far.*

and groups. It would be selfish of me to only pursue Street Pastors; God has called us not only in specific ways, but to be ready to work with like-minded people, people who are there for the good of the community and projects that are going in the same direction. This situation, right at the beginning of the Street Pastors initiative, when I could have been accused of wandering away from the embryonic work in London, was a valid opportunity for me to contribute some of my skills to CARISMA, even though it did not directly benefit Street Pastors.

One night Paul Keeble and I went out on the streets. We met fourteen-year-olds who talked about their bulletproof vests as if they were a normal part of their everyday clothing. Several groups of children were hanging around, and I recall one particular lad, a boy of eight years old, who was out with his friends. We asked him where his mother was and he replied, 'Don't worry about that bitch.' He told us he was with his brother, who was on the other side of the street in another gang. This child and his words stopped me from sleeping that night. What are the implications for us and our society, I wondered, when a child is out on the streets at that time of night?

As I talked to people I realised that many folk were grieving the loss of loved ones who had died through violence on the streets. This led Paul and me to organise a memorial service for those who had lost their lives to violence on the streets, and to acknowledge that, whatever their lifestyle had been, those people had family and friends who mourned them. It was obvious to us that there hadn't been any sort of recognition of their loss and that so many people had been touched by grief and pain. We wanted to recognise it but also 'draw a line and re-commit ourselves to taking positive action on behalf of our young people'.[3] We approached the cathedral and asked if we could hold the service there, as it represented neutral territory outside of the areas affected by gang rivalry.

At the cathedral we met with Canon Paul Denby. I was deeply impressed by him and the reception he gave to the idea. In advance of the memorial service we held a reception at the town hall for the families, to explain to them what we wanted to do and why, and to try to secure their involvement.

The day of the service came, in March 2003, and I was deeply moved to see the cathedral filling up. There was a roll call of all the names of the young men who had been shot and killed; in some cases brothers and members of the same family had died. Every time a name was called, a child from the audience brought out a daffodil and laid it on the altar. There must have been over fifty flowers lying there. Joel Edwards of the Evangelical Alliance lifted us out of the deep emotion of those moments with his encouraging message, and he was followed by the then bishop of Birmingham, who concluded the event with prayer. People thanked us for putting on this event, grateful that the church had remembered their plight and their sorrow and created the space for them to publicly grieve.

This event was another piece of the picture in my understanding of the problems for the community of South Manchester. We continued to have conversations with local congregations about the need for churches to respond and to work in partnership with others. Churches have a dual role to play: as a Christian presence, of course, but also to join with others to provide community cohesion.

---

3   Keeble, chapter 2, *CARISMA: History and Story So Far.*

However, it was difficult to convince churches to get out into Moss Side and Longsight, places where many high-profile killings had taken place over the years. Erinma Bell, whom I first met at one of the 'Guns on our streets' tour venues, was dedicated to the process of mapping the various groups and understanding the needs of the community. Though neither Erinma nor her husband Raymond were Christians, they both had a conviction to serve their community that was stronger than many Christians I had come across. Raymond was viewed as an elder in that community by many young people, and every time I met him he brought with him two or three young men that he was mentoring.

Finally we arrived at the point of voting for the organisational personnel for CARISMA. Like the first meeting, there was a massive turnout, including various local dignitaries and the media. Erinma Bell was voted in as chair, Paul Keeble as vice chair and a whole team of others to make up the rest of the organisation. In June 2007, CARISMA won the Queen's Award for Voluntary Service in recognition of the group's efforts to help the inner-city community rid their neighbourhood of gangs.[4]

After we had successfully launched CARISMA, we were able, after much persistence, to launch Street Pastors in Inner South Manchester in April 2004. The response from the local community was overwhelming. Many times I heard the words 'Glad to see you' or 'Glad to have you as a presence on the street'. Sometimes even, 'We're glad that Christians don't just go from home to church, church to home, but are

---

4   See *Manchester Evening News*, 25 June 2007. Erinma Bell was honoured for her work in 2008, when she was awarded an MBE by Gordon Brown. For the prime minister's comments see his book, *My Everyday Heroes* (Mainstream Publishing, 2007), an extract from which is available at Mail Online, www.dailymail.co.uk/femail.

willing to be involved with their communities.' Even a Rastafarian
saw the point: 'Pastor, on our streets today, prophecy is being ful-
filled ... the conflict of children against parents,' he commented as we
walked along late one night. 'But what excites me, pastor,' he went on,
'is that the church is willing to be salt and light.'

We still haven't got a large participation in Street Pastors among
the church membership in Moss Side today. This is in part because
Christians are nervous about the dangers on their streets. Yet a lot of
people who attend those churches will know, directly or indirectly,
someone who has been shot or killed or gone to prison because of
gun- or drug-related criminal activities. If all of us could say, as Patsy
McKie has said about the killing of her twenty-year-old son Dorrie in
a gang shooting, that her pain and her faith 'became a window into
Manchester society', our desire to put something back into our communities might be stronger.[5] Patsy is a lovely Christian woman. When
she telephoned me to tell me the news of her son's death in September
1999, I was deeply saddened. She had been leading a Bible club in her
church when she received a phone call to say that she must identify
her son's body at the hospital. Dorrie's death had massive implications
for Patsy and her family. It turned her life upside down. It was, for me,
another wake-up call from the communities that need us.

Once I was out there, I was fine ...

The first time I went out as a street pastor, we came
across a drunk young man who was suicidal. We talked

---

5   Patsy's words are part of her account of her son's death, as told in *Evangelicals Now*, December 2002, available at
    www.e-n.org.uk/p-2013-Mothers-against-violence.htm. Patsy is the chair of Mothers Against Violence.

to him and suggested that speaking to his mum might help. About a year later, as a team of us made our way down the now familiar hill towards the night clubs, we passed two young men. I was stopped by one of the men who wanted his mate to know, in no uncertain terms, what he thought about street pastors. During the next three minutes, he used the phrase, 'These guys saved my life', not once but three times.

Street pastor, Wrexham

The first night that I went out as a street pastor I introduced myself to a fish-and-chip-shop owner. He called to his assistant to take over and talked to me for twenty minutes. He told me he had worked in that neighbourhood all his life, but he was on the point of packing it all in. He described how knives had been pulled in his face, injured people had run into his shop for safety, women had been banging on his door screaming that they had been raped. His shop was literally across the road from the police station, but he still felt in danger. I encouraged him that good people should not give in to the bad things that go on in our society. He wanted to see change, but in his heart of hearts he didn't believe that change could happen. I think I was able to encourage him. I certainly enjoyed a portion of his fish and chips.

Street pastor, Lambeth

We walked on down to Kebab Planet (next to the Red Lion) and popped in to have a chat to the staff. It is part of our ministry to get to know and make ourselves known to all the people along the street and we are still making a first visit to many of these places. In common with most of the businesses open late at night, the staff do not speak English well, so we had a fragmentary conversation seeking to get across that we were there to help.

Street pastor, Sutton

My first night on duty was a 'baptism of fire'. We encountered a large group of young people emerging from a concert in the local recreation centre. Many of these young people were drunk and a serious fight broke out. We contacted the police, who were there in seconds and broke up the fight. However, as one of the ring leaders was being arrested, he managed to escape and jumped over a fence, down a bank and disappeared into a fast-flowing, swollen river. This resulted in a major incident, with fire engines and police helicopters trying to locate the missing lad.

We were involved in talking to other young people during the night as well as the boy's father, who came to the scene.

Street pastor, Bridgend

I was a bit apprehensive at first about going out but once out there I was fine. The thing that stood out for me the most was the conversation I had with a lady who was in her late twenties, in the pub on Meadow Street. I was at the bar ordering a coke and bag of crisps when she came up and stood next to me and started asking questions about who we were. Then she opened up and said she didn't believe in God. With deep sadness and pain in her eyes she went on to say that she had been born disabled and that she considered herself not to be pretty. She said if there was a God then why would He let her be born the way she was and have the life she'd had. She had been drinking but she wasn't drunk and she wasn't looking for an argument; she was just crying out. My heart went out to her with the love of God as we talked. I said I would pray for her and that I would be in the pub next Friday night to talk some more. I never thought one day I would be in a pub on Meadow Street at half eleven on a Friday night, wearing a big Street Pastor jacket, talking about Jesus. But I was that night. It was a fantastic night. I felt blessed and privileged to be there.

Street pastor, Preston and South Ribble

At the end of our first night out in March 2008 we met a policeman who was visiting his parents in the town. He leapt over the railings outside a large department store and asked who we were. After a long chat he volunteered the information that he was £10,000 in debt. He asked whether, if he prayed that night and asked Jesus to forgive him, Jesus would help him. Prayer was offered there and then, but the young man wanted to go home and give it some thought.

Street pastor, Torbay

CHAPTER TEN

ADOPT THE BANANA TEST
Caret, 2005

The challenges of growth

In their capacity as management consultants, an organisation called Caret have worked with Ascension Trust to help the Street Pastors initiative grow and evolve.[1] Among many other questions, challenges and assessments they have demanded from us, there was once an instruction to 'Adopt the banana test'. The banana test asks, 'When is a banana not a banana?' The reference originates in the EU's classification of bananas, with the 'banana test' being a reference to the separation of a true characteristic from a fake. As Street Pastors has expanded, with more volunteers, greater geographic spread and a stronger reputation, I have had to give time and attention to the challenges that growth brings.

---

1   www.caret.co.uk. Caret specialises in leadership and organisational growth. We are very grateful to the team at Caret for their work with us over several years, in particular Oliver Nyumbu, Marcus Cato, Jonathan Frank and Steve Botham.

Street Pastors is a model with values that need to be safeguarded and sustained on behalf of many more banana-eaters.

At Ascension Trust we haven't been able to build a structure fast enough to accommodate what God is doing. We cannot always keep up with God! One of the trustees once asked, with a twinkle in his eye, 'Can we not stop this thing, or slow it down?' My reply was, 'You talk to God about that!' We have had to recognise that God is at work.

We started with only eighteen street pastors deployed in the two boroughs of Hackney and Lambeth. Today the Ascension Trust office generally receives three inquiries a day from new areas looking to set up Street Pastors. We have experienced immense growth. We were excited when we reached one hundred fifty street pastors; thrilled when five hundred street pastors had gone through the training; amazed when we reached one thousand trained street pastors. Now we are heading for three thousand across one hundred twenty-five areas (at the time of writing), and as we give each of those areas some training twice a year, just that growth itself adds an enormous amount of work.

In contrast to the scepticism and cautiousness we received in the first few years, these days the Ascension Trust office might receive a phone call from a local police force, a city council or the centre manager of a town, and they ask, 'How can Street Pastors work with us?' We also take many calls from churches who want to start the initiative in their area, and we give them the information that they need and ensure that they make contact with the police in their town or city. We now find that many of the fears that council leaders or police officers held, that were evident in the early days of Street Pastors, have been allayed, partly by the good reports that circulate about us, and also often because the increased attitude of ownership *of* the community *by* the community speaks for itself. In Newham, East London, not so long ago, people were welcoming street pastors and hugging them. Had these been people with police authority, they would not have received the same reaction.

However, in 2004, as we started work in a third borough, Lewisham, the outlook was very daunting. Expansion was a spiritual and emotional drain, and our financial support was still uncertain. I remember saying to the trustees, 'If God is not in this, I'm quite prepared to pull the shutters down and go back to church leadership.' It was not easy to say, 'I trust the Lord and he will meet all my needs.' Thankfully, the Lord has consumed me with zeal to lead this initiative! A year or so before I gave up my pastoral responsibilities as a church leader I had spent time with Joel Edwards, then general secretary of the Evangelical Alliance, sharing with him my concerns for society and my vision to work with young people. Joel wisely saw that, to fulfil this role and the passion the Lord had birthed in me, I would need to be able to represent Street Pastors in high places, with government ministers, those in authority in the police force and leaders of the community.

Though I did not instinctively want to do this, I realised that it was a personal challenge I had to face. I would need to look two ways: towards the work on the ground, and towards the 'work in the air'—the interaction with policy makers to help them impact communities who need help. I would need to keep my feet on the ground but grow wings as well.

God in control

When God is moving, you are out of control and you have to trust Him. This is the first challenge. A significant way I can express my trust in God is to trust Him in the area of finance. In 2002, when Ascension Trust began to look at the Street Pastors concept, I recognised that with a project like this, we could find ourselves heavily reliant on government grants, local authority grants and the like. However, I was determined that we would not build on a foundation made of promises of money; I did not want to have to wait to receive money before we could start anything. I wanted Street Pastors to function even if there was no money coming in. The initiative was not based on receiving grants, it was based on people and their conviction to help their communities. We cannot put a price on loving people, showing charity to people or spending time with people. In our human, natural state, money plays an important role, but it should not be the bedrock of why we do what we do.

I also knew that we needed strong quality control and organisational procedures, but again, I did not want any of those things to drive the initiative. Understandably, this was a problem for Ascension Trust's trustees, who would have been happier if those things had been in place sooner.

If God is in control He will touch people—Christians or not—to give to this cause. 'God will meet all [our] needs according to his glorious riches' (Phil. 4:19). I am glad that we are always in need of money, because it means we keep trusting the Lord, seeking His guidance and relying on him to speak to people about supporting us financially. In reality this sometimes means that we are constrained by short-termism, unable to plan for the future. For instance, when we receive a grant for one year to employ someone, it's only a few months later that we have to start to think about the money for that person coming to an end, and this is far from ideal. Yet many individuals give generously to Street Pastors, and I thank the Lord for them.

The fact that when we train volunteers, we also ask them to give up their time and pay for their training and uniform always encourages me. There are so many other people who are also trusting in God for His provision! This underlines for me the fact that I am working with Christians who are ready to make a sacrifice for their community and their nation in obedience to the example set down by our Father God. 'For God so loved … he gave' (John 3:16). This is a Christ-centred attitude. What is, humanly speaking, a challenge is, biblically speaking, faith—total confidence in the Lord.

During the first two years of Street Pastors, I was on a massive learning curve, and so were the trustees. The Lord's provision for us was to bring people among us with the expertise and skills that we lacked. He heard us as we prayed for what we needed, and we have been blessed in so many ways by people who have helped us to grow and function. For example, as documented in chapter 7, many officers in the Metropolitan Police assisted us greatly in forming our standard operating procedures. Our consultants, Caret, had the expertise we needed to help us develop our structures, and the Jerusalem Trust gave us some money when we needed to dedicate resources to the formation of policies and procedures. God brought other people to us who could lift some of the burdens from me and start a distilling process with things that were crowding my mind.

At this stage I was very much eating, sleeping and dreaming Street Pastors. I had an office to run during the day, but I had street pastor duties on a Friday or Saturday night, as well as taking up opportunities to speak at community meetings and church events in the evening. Then there were the phone calls from communities asking one of us to come and patrol a specific area for a couple of nights because there were tensions there. The only thing that stopped me from feeling like I was spinning plates—going from one thing to another, giving just enough time and attention to stop something crashing to the ground—was my assurance that God was in control. Yet I was acutely aware of the rapid growth of the initiative, and in those early days I felt swamped.

After Lambeth, Hackney and Lewisham had set up teams, some London suburbs, like Kingston, came forward and expressed their interest in Street Pastors. How would we manage their expectations as well?

Mechanisms for growth

1. Procedures and quality control

As the initiative has developed, I have had to learn that the most important thing is not that we do everything at once, but that we understand what needs to be done now and set in place a procedure for working through everything else in due course. I have had to realise that I will not be able to do everything straightaway, but I know that I will do it in time. Good policies and procedures are essential because we are asking people to go out on the streets at night in situations that could make them very vulnerable. We want to ensure that people will commit to being a street pastor with confidence, having been trained with clear guidelines as to what they must or must not do, knowing how to act in the light of certain eventualities.

The training of street pastors has been a critical quality control and procedural waymarker. As our training programme matured and the number of people being trained grew, we started to become aware that the training needed to be moved on to another level in terms of standardisation and clarity. We also knew that our ethos could be presented more clearly, and if we were able to produce a training manual, then the baseline standards for training would be set and could be part of the package for all new Street Pastors teams. We received funding from the Home Office that enabled us to put the job of developing our training programme out to tender. Four training companies put in bids to help us write up our training into a manual and generally take on a consultant role for us.

As I sat around the table one afternoon with the trustees, listening to these companies make their pitch, I realised that I recognised one of the presenters, and after an initial inquiry, it transpired that we had met when he had acted as a trainer for speakers at Spring Harvest. His name was Oliver Nyumbu. His bid on behalf of a company called Caret was not the cheapest, but both I and the trustees felt that we should meet up with him to see whether what he was offering was very different from the cheaper bids. After further discussion, Oliver said that he liked what we were doing so much that he would reduce his fees because Street Pastors was 'kingdom stuff'. The trustees liked his expertise and his qualifications, which were very relevant for the work we wanted done.

As we finalised the timescale and outline for the project, Caret announced that they were going to take on the work free of charge—their board of directors had met together and agreed! We were given access to three of their top consultants who helped us to think about the growth and strengths of the organisation. This was a tremendous blessing, as major changes were taking place at Ascension Trust and we needed someone to advise us about managing change and growth. The team from Caret encouraged us to look to the future and to think about what kind of organisation we wanted to be in ten years' time. These were things we had barely had time to think about because we were so busy on the ground. Caret spent a year going through this process with us and, for me, it was an enormous blessing. The things that they helped us to think about and eventually do prevented administrative disasters as we grew. We are very grateful that they are still acting as our advisers.

2. Staffing

In the early stages we didn't have enough money to pay for staff; the people who worked for Ascension Trust had other part-time jobs to provide them with an income. I mentioned our need for someone to help with administration at one meeting and I was given the name of a woman called Janice Gittens. Janice has a lot of skills, and she agreed to come and work with us. We paid her what we could, but it wasn't much. That was the story all the way through. We have had a need and God has supplied the expertise.

Even now we only manage with the staff we have because everyone carries a very heavy workload. We are blessed with people of very high calibre and skills, who—praise God—see their work as ministry, with the compassionate desire to facilitate what God is doing through Street Pastors. This is true all over the country, where experienced people—such as Adrian Prior-Sankey, who has advised us about policies and procedures—are working with us to help us manage well what God has given us.

In Scotland, Martin Hill, Michael Archibald and James Duce are assisting us in the process of setting up Ascension Trust Scotland, through which the licence agreement for Street Pastors in that region will be operated. Differences in charity law have meant that an independent charitable body has been necessary in Scotland.

Many other people who are not part of the central staff have contributed to the development of Street Pastors in their locality. These people have a strong sense of ownership of Street Pastors, and they want to help us manage the initiative well. We have about fifteen Ascension Trust Representatives, men and women who represent a range of church denominations, and who are either coordinators or part of a management team. They have had training on our ethos, procedures and policies, and they are then able to go to any part of the country to give advice and help to set up a new team, lead a commissioning service, or a prepare a launch event. This tier of leadership has taken incredible pressures off me and the team in London. I am always really encouraged by the willingness of these people to serve.

3. Accountability

If something is going to have longevity, there must be a line of accountability. I feel very strongly that at each stage, accountability has to be paramount. Just as I am accountable to the board of trustees, it is important that every Street Pastors team has a clear line of accountability. All management teams, and the initiative as a whole, are accountable to the churches in the town or city in which they are set up, as well as to Ascension Trust. A coordinator is accountable to the management team. A senior street pastor is accountable to a coordinator. Each team is accountable to a senior street pastor. The initiative cannot be built on one person; that would be a recipe for disaster. There must be collective ownership and leadership of the initiative within an area.

4. Safety

We take people's safety very seriously. Street Pastors is not just about enthusiasm and passion, but about safety and the maintenance of our good reputation. If a street pastor were to get hurt in the course of their duties, the implications would be vast. As well as those who wish us well, sadly there are those who are waiting for something to go wrong so they can point the finger. It is very important that we do our utmost to prevent this from happening, particularly in these times when health and safety is such a big issue. We have gone to great lengths to establish proper procedural standards under guidance from the police, and have sought legal advice about what street pastors should do in various scenarios.

Our training is vital in teaching people how to read a situation and recognise when to walk away. Knowing how to deal with someone who is intoxicated is critical. When someone is drunk they are unpredictable; they might do anything. As much as you or I want to help that individual, we have to display some skill in how we do it.

On one occasion I saw street pastors trying to help a man who was staggering down the road. They asked him, 'Are you okay?' He said, 'Go away.' The team kept their distance but did not lose sight of him. Shortly afterwards he collapsed, and the street pastors realised that he had, in fact, been stabbed. They called an ambulance, kept him talking while they waited for it to arrive, asked if there was someone they could phone for him, and were eventually able to inform a relative which hospital he had been taken to. They stayed outside the zone of risk and danger, but they were still of use to the man.

On another occasion I was in a pub and was on the receiving end of some choice words from a man who obviously wished I wasn't there. I left him alone and got out of his space. I knew he wasn't angry with me—he didn't even know me. Forty minutes later he came over and apologised to me, offered to buy me a drink, and explained that he had once had a bad experience with his priest. Street pastors must be able to assess the situation and respond accordingly.

We are constantly developing our risk-assessment skills and keeping our eyes on the ball. This was something that, right from the start, DC Ian Crichlow drew our attention to. I just wanted to get things done, but he made me realise that we have so much to lose if something goes wrong on the street. In some areas street pastors have a radio mike with a headpiece and they work very closely with CCTV operators who are in contact with the police. However, in other places—generally the major cities—teams don't use radios because it smacks of authority.

In one area street pastors were talking to a guy when his mate ran up, saying that another of their friends was getting into a fight. The street pastors calmed both young men and encouraged them not to get involved. Seeing that the conflict was still brewing, they phoned the police, who said, 'Don't worry, we've been watching the situation, and you, for the last ten minutes.' Prayer, procedure and CCTV: street pastors are covered from all angles!

> At 3.45 a.m. the street pastors were tapped on the shoulder by a sober young woman who explained that she had been walking home to her house in a nearby terraced street but found herself being stalked by a strange young man on a bicycle. The team escorted her home safely, but as she disappeared through her front door the chap on the bike came into view again at the top of her street, circling around to see where she might have gone. We radioed through to camera control and our conversation, asking for them to track the cyclist, was picked up by the town centre beat manager.
>
> *Street pastor, Taunton*

5. Standardisation

Over the years we have been advised of a couple of areas where churches or other groups have set up Street Pastors teams without coming to us. Essentially, they have copied us but not wanted to be part of the larger Street Pastors family of which we are the hub.

I don't really get troubled by this; there is enough work out there for all of us. However, if you are not part of the Street Pastors family you have not been trained by us and you are not covered by insurance. Furthermore, it is essential that we keep control over the image of Street Pastors and the activities of the people who go out under our banner—if an untrained street pastor happened to act inappropriately it would affect every other scheme throughout the country. That is why 'Street Pastors' is a registered trademark of Ascension Trust.

Occasionally, we have had to have a quiet chat with someone who is a 'loose cannon' like this. We always try to get such people on board, but some resist. Technically, these groups or individuals are breaking the law, because they are using our trademarked name without permission. But even more of a concern is the potential for bringing the whole scheme into disrepute, so we take this very seriously. Every street pastor is accountable to others.

If a group doesn't want to be part of the national network, and if they have got people willing to do things, then that's great; but please don't break the law. Only those areas appearing on our website are bona fide Street Pastors teams.

Despite the big legal and procedural building blocks we have taken on, we want to remain faithful to our small beginnings—churches responding to what is happening in their communities. Even so, structures help many who are not Christians to feel they can work with us. Some people respond well to structures and some don't. The police like structure ... local authorities like structure ... let's be honest, churches like structure! As a network for learning, support and growth, we shouldn't undervalue it. The

Lord is doing something with us and through us. The challenge for us is always to ask how we are to manage it properly. When a town or city comes to us with the will to set up a Street Pastors team, what do we need to put in place for them? When I talk about the challenges of growth, our focus has never been 'where next?' It has always been to manage, to the best of our ability, the teams that come to us.

How do we stop Street Pastors becoming another wave on the beach of Christian social action? If I say anything about Street Pastors, it is this: The Lord is doing something here. So, to follow that to its natural conclusion, when the Lord stops moving, so do we. There are enormous challenges in many ways for us, but if the Lord is doing it, if the Lord builds, then we do not labour in vain (Ps. 127:1). Whatever the Lord does is good. He has a bigger purpose. When He stops, we can draw a line under it and say 'Amen!' People say to us that our marketing has been excellent; I think to myself, what are they talking about? It is the Lord who does it! Street Pastors is what the Lord is doing, and it is marvellous in our eyes! (See Matt. 21:42.) Whatever I have wanted to see happen, the Lord has done it ten times bigger and better ... and I am left saying, 'Wow!'

International growth

It was obvious to all of us within the first two years of the life of the initiative that Street Pastors had the potential to go far. Although I have always seen the possibility for international growth, there was so much to learn that it has not come onto the agenda until relatively recently. There are so many implications to expanding into other countries, just like the legal issues and quality control demands of establishing the hub of Street Pastors in the UK, only bigger and even more challenging. For a long time it was clearly too difficult because of all the other pressures. However, three years after the birth of Street Pastors, things began to happen.

Antigua is my place of birth. On one of my frequent visits to the island, in January 2005, I met a local church leader and told him about the initiative. He was interested enough to suggest that we talk to some other church leaders about it. When I returned to Antigua in June that year, I took with me Chief Inspector Leroy Logan, Revd Katie Kirby (general director of the African and Caribbean Evangelical Alliance), Revd Jimi Adeleye and Chris Ekhator. The purpose of our visit was to lead a one-day conference on the concept of Street Pastors, and to meet a variety of church leaders and representatives from the police.

This was not just another conference: The keynote speaker was the Honourable Baldwin Spencer, the prime minister! The prime minister liked the sound of what we said and introduced us to his colleague, the Honourable Hilson Baptiste, the minister of Housing, Culture and Social Transformation, who also fully endorsed the initiative. I was quite taken aback. It was almost as if he had the vision and the concept in his mind before we spoke it.

Churches in Antigua were excited and cautious in equal measures. It was decided that a delegation would be assembled to visit England to see the initiative at work, to meet with the police and local government, and to attend a Street Pastors training course. The following year, in September 2006, two police officers, two civil servants and three church leaders from Antigua arrived in London.

The Antiguan ambassador in Britain, Dr Carl Roberts, coordinated a conference at Southwark Town Hall for the Antiguan delegation and local street pastors. This visit also included meetings with the mayor of Lambeth and the opportunity to accompany the police in Hackney and Southwark. The Antiguan visitors left this country with a lot of enthusiasm to start up Street Pastors in Antigua.

After Eustace and Sharon Constance had led the training for the Antiguan team, the initiative was launched in January 2007. The Antiguan government gave us office space (the top floor of a two-story building) and the use of a vehicle, together with a salary for a coordinator. Two big challenges to the successful operation of the initiative in Antigua presented themselves. The first one was that those who had agreed to be on the management team were all busy people—either police officers, church leaders or civil servants—and as they were constrained by their workloads they were not in a position to implement the decisions we had made. Second, the concept of volunteering and paying for training and a uniform was something of a cultural hurdle. People were cautious about volunteering, and we were also finding it hard to appoint a coordinator. I felt that we needed to find people in England who would be willing to go to Antigua to fill that role.

I sent out an e-mail across the Street Pastors community, and within a couple of weeks received a reply from one of our coordinators in Norwich, containing the names of a couple who might be the right ones for the job: Paula and Martin Callam. They had had their hearts set on Christian work in Bosnia, but their plans had recently fallen through. They were disappointed at the time, but what they hadn't realised was that the hand of God was in that to keep them available for Street Pastors in Antigua. Paula and Martin are our first overseas workers.

We have received enquiries from all over the world, including Australia, Canada, New Zealand, Nigeria, Guyana and America. I am not consciously developing the international profile of Street Pastors, but if it happens, it happens. If asked, I feel I am ready to talk to people now about the international picture, because I know that God is touching people's hearts about communities all around the world.

APPENDIX

SETTING UP A STREET PASTORS TEAM

'Street Pastors' proposed for Weston

What goes on in our town centre in the evenings and at night times up to 4 a.m., especially at weekends? A meeting at Milton Baptist Church last month, entitled 'Church involvement in the night economy of Weston-super-Mare' set out to give an answer.

At the meeting attended by more than 100 people, police sergeants gave a graphic picture of the problems faced by the NHS and the police; also the future risks to the health and welfare of young people's binge drinking, and costs to the public. The cost of taking a drunkenness or assault case through to sentencing is a staggering £190,000. And on one night there could be up to twenty arrests in the town.

A spokesman from the Church Army said churches need to be involved. 'God loves these folk and they are in great need. They would not come to us. We have to go to them.' He spoke of a Street Pastors scheme that has been very effective in London, Birmingham, Manchester and Southend.

As a result of interest generated, a follow-up meeting was held to consider the church's response. After this second meeting it was said that 'support from the two meetings confirmed that it would be right to continue to develop the Street Pastors project in Weston'.

It was agreed that a working party should be formed and that the Revd Les Isaac be invited to the town to speak on the project.

Churches Together, *Weston-super-Mare, Spring 2006*

The licence agreement between Ascension Trust and a local Street Pastors team was introduced in 2005, when Street Pastors was operating in five locations. It is a document of understanding and expectations, signed by each management committee at the outset of our partnership with a team. The relationship between the 'hub', Ascension Trust, and each local Street Pastors team is fundamental to the success of the work. The licence agreement outlines the way in which that relationship will work, and defines the commitments that the Trust makes to local Street Pastors teams, and the behaviour expected from them.

Whenever an area has signed a licence agreement, it is also signed by the trustees and by me. We then set up an e-mail address for them, they receive a copy of the agreement, a copy of the certificate of association and an insurance document. They will also receive from us a coordinator's pack, plus logos and documents about processes and procedures. These include protocols for dealing with vulnerable adults, child protection issues, employment documents (a job description and guidelines regarding payment of a coordinator), reference documents and volunteer agreements. There is also a code of practice, explaining what is acceptable and what is not for a street pastor. It is all designed to bring clarity, and it is our responsibility to ensure that each team has all this information and protection.

All volunteers going out onto the streets must wear the distinctive Street Pastors uniform, and this is also a fixed part of the agreement. The uniform is essential to our identity on the streets, our approachability and the ease with which street pastors can be identified on CCTV and by police officers. All trained and commissioned volunteers must wear the Street Pastors jacket and cap (other items are optional) when they are on duty.

> When I first heard about Street Pastors, it was something I didn't like the idea of. I am an evangelist and I am out on the streets all the time, so I wasn't keen, in particular, on the idea of a uniform because I thought it would stop me from being a part of the real community. Now I see that the uniform represents the physical presence of the church and the image has got a good reputation.
>
> *Street pastor, Inner South Manchester*

One of the most challenging things about the licence agreement for us at Ascension Trust is the management licence fee. This is an expectation that each year the local Street Pastors organisation will pay to the Trust a 15 percent management fee, calculated as a proportion of the overall income of the local initiative.

Up to the point at which we developed the agreement, there was no financial relationship between us and a local team. Sustaining the growth of Street Pastors would be an enormous strain without some money coming back to us from individual teams, money that supports us in the delivery of the work nationally. The management fee produced a number of different responses from our partners: some, especially the police and local authorities, appreciated the need for it, and so did a good proportion of the churches; but it was a foreign language to others. It needed much discussion.

The management fee is not a condition of the continuing relationship between Ascension Trust and a Street Pastors team. If your team does not receive a penny from anywhere (local churches, police, council, community organisations) you will still receive 100 percent of our resources. It is a kingdom principle that those who are able to should support others; those who don't have an income will get the same from us as those that do, because the Trust exists to equip the church to serve its community.

The point at which a management committee starts to meet with the police and local government officers is a good time to investigate the possibility of funding through these partners. Frank and open conversations, in which costs are attached to things such as office space and secretarial support, are encouraged. Relationships with churches should be consistent and ongoing, and churches should play their part financially.

I called a meeting of local Christians who might be interested in working with me to launch a Street Pastors scheme in Taunton. I was amazed that twenty people turned out on a cold night in January and even more surprised when, in response to my appeal for people willing to put their shoulder to the wheel and help with administration, three people came forward.

Shortly afterwards a cheque for £200 was sent to me by the local police district. It seems they had heard of the efforts being made to start a Street Pastors scheme and simply wanted to offer some practical encouragement.

Street pastor, Taunton

So the licence agreement helped to move us away from the organic relationship we had with Street Pastors teams in the beginning towards a more clearly defined, quantifiable partnership. Again we greatly benefited from our consultants Caret in the process of putting together this document. It became clear to us and to Caret that part of the rationale behind the agreement was the need to highlight key principles about the ethos of Street Pastors. These fixed principles contain the nature of our work. The fixed principles say that our aim is to listen, care and help. We are nonjudgmental and will give time and love to anyone. They remind us that we are not street pastors because we want to preach, but because we want to integrate people into society.

The concept of the urban trinity is fundamental to the operations of Street Pastors, and is another fixed principle emphasised in the licence agreement. We want to articulate the fact that no single organisation can tackle the problems we face in the twenty-first century. No one church, no one social service department. The first level of partnership that we need is for churches to pray together, work together and overcome traditional and denominational differences together. They have to find a common ground, which I believe is the cross, and start from there. Together churches can do a far better job than if they work in isolation.

When you start something on a local level there is always a risk that, by the time it reaches a national level, it will have mutated into something different. Therefore, Ascension Trust has a number of expectations that a Street Pastors team must comply with before it is able to start the training programme.

Here are a few of the requirements we set in place:

- Local teams are formed by a cross-denominational group of at least four churches.

- There is partnership with local police and local government.

- The training and selection of street pastors adheres to the guidelines.[1]

A prison governor once said to me that he would like to have street pastors on every wing of his prison, because he was getting good reports from inmates about encounters they had had with street pastors before they were convicted. What would be the effect, I

---

1   Volunteers must be over the age of eighteen, must have a reference from a church leader, must have cleared a Criminal Records Bureau check and have completed the Street Pastors training course. Team coordinators make a careful selection of volunteers and reserve the right to say, after training, that someone is not yet ready to go out on the streets.

sometimes worry, if someone were to have a bad experience of Street Pastors?

This is another way in which the management fee enables quality control to take place. It communicates to a local team that the 'brand' they have from us is only on loan: we can stop them from operating if we need to. With the management fee and the licence agreement comes the imperative and the opportunity for Ascension Trust to manage better and keep our eyes fixed on what is happening nationally.

For more information, please visit our website:

www.streetpastors.co.uk

or email:

info@streetpastors.org.uk

or telephone the London office:

(+44) (0)207 771 9770